BEYOND

COMPARE

BEYOND COMPARE

Moving Past the Habit That Holds You Back

Kristen White

Beyond Compare
© 2020 Kristen White

Kristen White
P.O. Box 654
Shelbyville, Ky. 40066
www.womenwithroots.com

ISBN: 978-1-09834-731-4 Paperback
ISBN: 978-1-09834-732-1 eBook
First Edition
Printed in the U.S.A.

DEDICATION

For Dennis and Sue,
Barbara, and Julie.
Thank you for showing me that
the love of Jesus is beyond compare.

CONTENTS

Part 1

So You Want to Be a Superhero
An Honest Look at Comparison

Part 2

You Make Me Sick
What Comparison Is Doing Inside

Part 3

Who's the Real Hero?
How Jesus Sets Us Free from Comparison

Part 4

Redefined

LAUGH at Satan's Lies

Part 5

Watch for Ivy

Know What You're Choosing

Part 6

Looking for Oaks

Finding Peace and Purpose

Getting Started

Let's be honest about something. Our thought life isn't always sunshine, roses, and glitter. Sometimes we're eaten up with jealousy and insecurity and we can't stop ourselves from comparison.

Comparison is supposed to be helpful, right? Like, if you were in the produce aisle, you would pick a perfectly shaped, bright green watermelon over a lumpy one with soft brown spots. If you were on a game show, you'd choose a new car over a lifetime supply of mac and cheese. Maybe that depends on how much you love mac and cheese. ☺

The thing is, people are not produce or prizes. It's natural to compare. Comparison swells inside us because we have hearts that want to fit in and souls that want to be loved. There's nothing sinful about this drive to find significance. God uses it to help us find Him. Unchecked, though, comparison can take us to a dark place.

We start simply enough, glancing to the side, noticing people who are "better" than us. "They have it all together," we think. Then the conclusion becomes, "I don't." Without meaning to, we trade the real truths that we are loved and special for the idea that we aren't. Thought patterns nibble their way in like termites, eat up our vibrancy, and leave the dust of sadness and regret. The way to stop this intruder is to recognize that real significance doesn't come from being superior. It doesn't even come from being special. Significance comes from knowing God and His Son. It is beautiful that He has invited us to do that.

During our journey together, we'll look at different aspects of comparison. We'll look at real people in the Bible who were misled by their thoughts. Full disclosure: you're gonna see some nastiness. I'm going to ask you to be honest about your memories and motivations, and I will be, too, as we wrestle for God to lead our thought lives and deepen our belief in His love.

I encourage you to spend time on this book every day for the duration. Don't feel pressured to finish a chapter each day—even a few minutes can help reset your mind and bring you peace. A small amount of time out of the next couple of months isn't much to give for a closer walk with God. Instead of spending 20 minutes on social media, spend 20 minutes with Jesus.

For your convenience, I included the focus Bible passage at the beginning of each chapter. Take time to read these. They are the foundation for all we're learning. Even better, open your Bible and read the entire chapter. Mark what stands out. Journal how God is speaking to you. Memorize verses—post them on your mirror. And tell others—friends, mentors—what you're learning. Verbalizing God's truths helps fix them in your brain.

This book is a result of my own struggles and how God stepped in, spoke to my heart, and rescued me with His Word. I know He is going to speak to you, too. He promises He will (Isaiah 55:11, Hebrews 4:12).

Are you ready to move beyond compare? Let's go!

Part 1

SO YOU WANT TO BE A SUPERHERO?

An Honest Look at Comparison

"God chose the foolish things of the world to shame the
wise. God chose the weak things of the world to shame
the strong. God chose the things of this world that are
common and looked down on. God chose things
considered unimportant to do away with things
considered important. So no one can boast to God.
Because of what God has done,
you belong to Christ Jesus."
1 Corinthians 1:27-30, NIrV

Beginning Thoughts

We all love a good superhero movie, where good triumphs over evil and someone epic steps in to protect the underdog. None of us would say we are looking to *be* a superhero. But when we compare ourselves to other people, we may be looking for superhuman qualities more than we realize. We are trying to find what would make us better than we currently are. Maybe even better than other people.

That's not how we think of it! We don't want to be superior. We only want to know we are significant.

That's how comparison starts. But is that how it ends? Our search for *super* is causing pain we didn't realize. Instead of giving us confidence, it gives us anxiety.

In this part we will use fun analogies about superheroes to look at how comparison gets started. We will learn what we are really saying about God, others, and ourselves when we compare. And we'll start to see how we can stop this habit that's holding us back.

TAKEAWAYS FOR PART 1
- Most of us struggle with comparing ourselves to others.
- We compare because we are searching for a place to belong and the assurance that we are important.
- You don't have to be perfect to be the genuine, remarkable woman God wants you to be.

CHAPTER 1
As Good as God?
Comparison makes us want *more*.

Now the serpent was more crafty than any other beast of the field that the Lord God had made.

He said to the woman, "Did God actually say, 'You shall not eat of any tree in the garden'?" And the woman said to the serpent, "We may eat of the fruit of the trees in the garden, but God said, 'You shall not eat of the fruit of the tree that is in the midst of the garden, neither shall you touch it, lest you die.'" But the serpent said to the woman, "You will not surely die. For God knows that when you eat of it your eyes will be opened, and you will be like God, knowing good and evil." So when the woman saw that the tree was good for food, and that it was a delight to the eyes, and that the tree was to be desired to make one wise, she took of its fruit and ate, and she also gave some to her husband who was with her, and he ate. Then the eyes of both were opened, and they knew that they were naked.

Genesis 3:1-7

Want to hear one of the saddest things ever? One time, my family went camping at a place with a pool. My little girl hit the filter box lid with her toe when I lifted her out of the pool. The lid popped off, and she squealed and started crying. I thought she was hurt, but she pointed to the filter basket. Inside was a baby bunny. He had gotten stuck in the water and drowned. We were all very distressed. That bunny should have had a long, good life. He didn't belong in the water.

For a moment, think of comparison as tossing stuff into pure, clean water. You would not throw buckets of dirt into your neighborhood pool. You would never empty a bag of trash into a pristine cove on the coast of Hawaii. But we throw comparisons in the water of our life all day long. Think of all the things you have that, when you put them beside other people's stuff, don't seem good enough. Think of the list of things you wish you had—not only material possessions, but circumstances, relationships, talents, and experiences. What did you throw in the water this week? Maybe a great Instagram feed. Popularity. A pair of shoes. A test score. The boy you wish would pay attention to you. A friend's sense of humor. A Spring Break trip. People you wanted great relationships with, maybe a dad or a best friend.

Our life water gets crowded fast. If you look around for a quick minute, you will find something you wish you had— cash, cars, cuteness. The things others have can make us feel inadequate. Behind. We think it doesn't hurt to want the good stuff other people has, but it causes brokenness. Why do we do it? I think we mistakenly assume that comparison helps us improve. If we improve, we'll be better liked. When will we see that's not true, and why do we need to be liked so much?

All human beings want to belong. Everyone needs to feel valid. This need for significance isn't wrong or shameful; it's a beautiful, natural part of being human. We don't apologize for having physical needs like food and water; to live, we must eat. We get that. Sometimes we feel guilty for having emotional needs, but they are not a sign of weakness. God designed our need to belong for a reason. He wants us to find that He fulfills it.

Needing approval, wanting to belong, even wanting nice things, these are as innate as breathing. How we search for them, where we find them, and how much power we give them to make us feel satisfied, that's what gets us into trouble. Where we go wrong is mistaking superiority for significance—thinking we have to be *better* to be valuable.

We want *more*. We want it *now*. If we don't get it, we will be discontent. What is at the root of the dissatisfaction and fear that drive us every day? Let's name insecurity if that's what we're struggling with. And let's name selfishness or anything else that's keeping us from confidence.

Comparison isn't always evaluating yourself alongside another person. Sometimes it is holding your experience up against expectations—life wasn't supposed to be this hard. This disappointing. Sometimes comparison is holding your life up against God's limitless power—He *could* do or give more, so why isn't He? We become convinced that if we had more than we currently do, we'd be more content: more stuff, more admiration, more in the bank. We are determined to find that *more* above everything else.

At the beginning, Adam and Eve fell into wanting more without even realizing it. Think about it, everywhere Eve looked, she saw unblemished beauty. The food was delicious. Her hair was not riddled with split ends. She lived in absolute perfection because, before sin, no kind of decay was in the world. Nothing was wrong. Eve lived without fear and with

14

absolute security that she would have everything she needed for a safe, whole life. If she had not rebelled against God, sin would not have entered the world, and she never would have died. She would have walked in unbroken and communication with God and her spouse forever.

But Eve traded all she had for the *more* that the Deceiver promised her: "No! You will not die," the serpent said to the woman. "In fact, God knows that when you eat the fruit, your eyes will be opened and you will be like God, knowing good and evil." Satan convinced her that she did not have enough—God was withholding. She decided to trade her beautiful life and risk sudden death for the chance of more superiority, for the chance to be ... superhuman. Then she'd really be amazing. She'd be like God.

If you asked Eve in that moment of decision whether she wanted to be as good as God, she'd probably say, "No way." Yet she gave in to Satan's appeal to become like God. (Funny, in the very conversation he made being *like* God sound so appealing, he also made the person of God sound mean, stingy, and limiting.)

NEVER ENOUGH

In what areas do you feel like you're not good enough? Circle the ones you struggle with most.

Money	Smarts
Accomplishments	Beauty
Personality	Body
Wardrobe	Guys
Health/energy level	Spiritual growth
Social media influence	Popularity

We're still struggling with the same old game. Our full-of-blessing lives seem inferior when we compare. If we're not careful, we come to the grumpy conclusions that we don't have enough, aren't enough to make a difference, life is unfair, and God is mean. When we get in the habit of comparison, we trade contentment for anxiety. We end up fearing that we are missing out.

In the moment of temptation, the Deceiver told Eve there was more—that if she ate the fruit, she would be like God, knowing good and evil. She already knew good. She knew God. What partaking of the fruit introduced into her life (and the entire world) was evil. Chaos. Death. Darkness. Sin and its inescapable consequences. Satan was convincing, and Eve's fear that she was missing out got us more trouble than we know what to do with!

Go back and take a look at the list of all the areas in which you feel inferior (pg. 15). If you could suddenly have piles of money, clothes, and popularity, would you really have what your heart wants? If you were extraordinarily gifted in a favorite area, would that be enough? I don't think we really want to be superhuman. We don't want to be responsible for that much. What we really want, what the human soul desires most, is significance—approval, attention, the ability to bless others. So where is the right place to find it?

You can know for sure that God has decided you are indescribably important. Jesus paid for our souls with His life. In coming chapters, we will come face to face with how deeply that impacts our worth and freedom.

She is so pretty and skinny. Her style is amazing. She gets so many likes on her posts. Everyone thinks she's so sweet. They seem to have such a warm, deep friendship. Every boy asks for her Snapchat. If you are like me, plenty of stuff is floating around in your life's water. If I am honest, it is sad how insecure and dissatisfied I am and how much more I want.

Who told us our lives weren't enough to be content? Your whole life can be built upon the foundational truth that you are important to the Most Important One, or it can be spent looking for importance in non-lasting ways and imperfect people. I pray we will learn to trust that God's love is more than enough to satisfy us, instead of trying to be superhuman without Him.

CHAPTER 2
X-Ray Vision

Comparison keeps our eyes on the wrong road.

Now Adam knew Eve his wife, and she conceived and bore Cain, saying, "I have gotten a man with the help of the Lord." And again, she bore his brother Abel. Now Abel was a keeper of sheep, and Cain a worker of the ground. In the course of time Cain brought to the Lord an offering of the fruit of the ground, and Abel also brought of the firstborn of his flock and of their fat portions. And the Lord had regard for Abel and his offering, but for Cain and his offering he had no regard. So Cain was very angry, and his face fell. The Lord said to Cain, "Why are you angry, and why has your face fallen? If you do well, will you not be accepted? And if you do not do well, sin is crouching at the door. Its desire is contrary to you, but you must rule over it."

Cain spoke to Abel his brother. And when they were in the field, Cain rose up against his brother Abel and killed him. Then the Lord said to Cain, "Where is Abel your brother?" He said, "I do not know; am I my brother's keeper?" And the Lord said, "What have you done? The voice of your brother's blood is crying to me from the ground. And now you are cursed from the ground, which has opened its mouth to receive your brother's blood from your hand.

Genesis 4:1-11

You've heard of superheroes having x-ray or night vision. You've probably heard that chameleons have a 360 degree range of vision. They can turn their beady eyes all the way around. When we compare, sometimes we get this feeling that we have exclusive vision, too—that if we gaze long and hard at others or our phone, we will see what it takes to be special. In reality, comparison makes us see God, people, and ourselves with *inaccurate* clarity.

Comparison is like looking in a rearview mirror. Your eyes are focused on the people coming up behind you. You notice their fancy car, devices, or clothes. You feel deflated when they pass you. Even though comparison promises to make us "better," we always end up feeling *worse*—like we are left out. The glance in your rearview mirror before you change lanes is meant to broaden your view, not become it. If you look only at the rearview mirror when you drive down the road, you will crash into something in front of you. That's not "exclusive" vision—that's not keeping your eye on the road.

Here's an extreme example: You leave school to head to your job at the mall, when *the girl* (the one it's difficult not to compare yourself to) pulls up behind you. Every guy at school talks about her perfect body. All she talks about is working out. She passes you in her zippy new car when the light turns green. What do you do? You follow her to her gym. You check in, like this is something you do every day. You crank the elliptical as fast as you can and lift weights. You use muscles you never knew you had. When you're done, your whole body is throbbing and she smirks a half-approving, half-sarcastic smile and says, "Pretty good for someone who doesn't work out." You realize you missed work, dinner with your family, and hanging out with your little sister who loves you—and for what?

Okay, we'd never literally follow someone. That's a little creepy. But don't we sort of do that when we take cues from *the girl* when deciding what to wear, what to post, who to hang out with, or what to do on the weekend? Have you ever decided to buy or do something, not because it was your favorite, but because you felt you needed to do that to fit in or be liked? Our thinking becomes unhealthy when we look at others too long. When our eyes are not fixed on Jesus, we forget the truth that He created our uniqueness. We may mistakenly conclude that if we are not good at the things others are good at, we aren't good at all.

When we take our eyes off God's plan for us, we keep readjusting our destination. Looking in the rearview mirror, we make decisions based on whether or not we'll be liked or feel competent enough, rather than on what God wants us to do. That's called being *peer dependent*. When we follow our insecurities rather than God, we will unintentionally choose our way, one people-pleasing decision at a time, to a dangerous destination.

It feels innocent—and sometimes it is—to mimic those we admire. But when we are convinced that everyone around us is "better," and we decide to do whatever it takes to play catch-up, we tread in places God never wanted us to go.

Here's another extreme example. Unfortunately, it is a true story. Cain and Abel, Adam and Eve's first two children, grew up knowing about Almighty God. When they were young adults, they presented gifts to God to acknowledge and thank Him. God accepted Abel's offering but not Cain's. Was God playing favorites? No, when God rejected Cain's offering, He didn't do so without basis. His care for people isn't conditional and random. Scripture tells us why God didn't receive Cain's offering: it *wasn't* an act of worship.

20

It was an act of obligation. Verse 3 uses no descriptive words for Cain's gift; merely calls it "some" produce. The purpose God has for offerings—special sacrificial gifts we give to God's work—is to help us unclench our fists on what we own and recognize that He is greater than earthly things. When we make an offering, we are saying that God is a bigger deal than anything else in our lives. We adore Him. At the heart of a true offering is a heart that is ready to submit to God's authority. People give stuff that looks like an offering all the time—they write a check or volunteer their time—but God sees more than the item given. He sees *how* the item is given. And He saw that Cain's heart was self-focused. Cain gave the offering to look good himself, rather than to acknowledge that God was the only good One.

When God called Cain out for his improperly-offered gift, He wasn't being cruel and reject-y. He was actually being kind. He reached out to Him with grace and gave him a second chance to draw close to God. He spoke to Cain and urged him to learn from his mistake. God wasn't withholding approval and shouting, "It is impossible for you to measure up!" He was saying, "Let's try this again. I want your heart to know me."

It was Cain's *offering* that didn't measure up, not his intrinsic worth. His offering showed a heart that didn't care about God. God wanted more for Cain than that. But Cain didn't take God's correction as gracious. He took it as rejection. Why did Cain have such a problem being corrected? Why do we?

When unaddressed insecurity lives inside, it grows and does its destructive work. Like undetected cancer, we may not know it is there. But if someone addresses a root connected to our insecurity, a trigger gets tripped. The most common

21

explosion that bursts out of us is *blame*. When God confronted Cain, he was already in the habit of comparing himself with his brother. So instead of accepting responsibility and saying, "You're right, God. I am struggling with jealousy and selfishness. Please change my heart," Cain turned his fury on his brother. Cain blamed his brother for his personal distance from God. The truth was, friendship with God was always available. The truth was, Abel's offering had nothing to do with God's rejection of Cain's. God wasn't comparing the brothers. He was looking at each individual heart (see 1 John 3:11-12 for more explanation about the attitude in Cain's heart). Even after hearing God's gentle voice, Cain made a terribly misdirected decision. His jealousy drove him to annihilate Abel. He didn't even consider that he was choosing more distance from God and that, this time, the consequences would be even heavier to bear.

SAY *NO* TO SIN

You do not have to do or say every thought that comes into your mind. When Cain stewed and brewed in his anger, God spoke truth to him that we also need to know: we **can** say no to sin. God's message is opposite the message of our "you do you" culture. We're told, "Follow your heart. Do what makes you happy." Should we really live with no thought of anything but our own desires? With the help of the Holy Spirit, every believer has the ability to resist evil and do good. It's really hard to say no to yourself—people don't like to bend their will and submit to a holy God they can't see. Ask Him for strength to follow Him well.

Here is a truth we keep missing: We are not competing for God's love. There is not one tiny little prize that's going to be awarded to one person in your church, city, and generation. There is not one "best in show." There's enough of Jesus to go around.

So what are you looking for in the rearview mirror? If you are basing every decision on the limited picture you get in the blurry reflection of comparison, let me encourage you. Take some time to close your eyes in prayer. Fix your eyes upward—on the One who holds your life in His hands.

WE NEED ALL Y'ALL

Do you sometimes think only one person can be good at singing, photography, or something you'd like to be good at? So when someone you know is "better" than you at the thing you enjoy, you shrink back and stop trying? Society needs multiple people in every town doing most jobs. The world couldn't run if there weren't *many* skilled builders, doctors, computer programmers, grocers, teachers, artists, musicians, cleaners, accountants, and service providers of all kinds. **Every person counts**, and every person will make a unique impact on their circle. Every day, you can get up and go with God's confidence because *we need you!*

CHAPTER 3
Swiss-Army Limbs
Comparison makes us want others' happiness.

Then two prostitutes came to the king and stood before [King Solomon]. The one woman said, "Oh, my lord, this woman and I live in the same house, and I gave birth to a child while she was in the house. Then on the third day after I gave birth, this woman also gave birth. And we were alone...in the house.... And this woman's son died in the night, because she lay on him. And she arose at midnight and took my son from beside me, while your servant slept, and laid him at her breast, and laid her dead son at my breast. When I rose in the morning to nurse my child, behold, he was dead. But when I looked at him closely in the morning, behold, he was not the child that I had borne." But the other woman said, "No, the living child is mine, and the dead child is yours." The first said, "No, the dead child is yours, and the living child is mine." Thus they spoke before the king....

And the king said, "Bring me a sword." So a sword was brought before the king. And the king said, "Divide the living child in two, and give half to the one and half to the other." Then the woman whose son was alive said to the king, because her heart yearned for her son, "Oh, my lord, give her the living child, and by no means put him to death." But the other said, "He shall be neither mine nor yours; divide him." Then the king answered and said, "Give the living child to the first woman, and by no means put him to death; she is his mother." And all Israel heard of the judgment that the king had rendered, and they stood in awe of the king, because they perceived that the wisdom of God was in him to do justice.

1 Kings 3:16-28

What if you could whip out a phone charger, nail clippers, or tire jack if a friend needed it—tuck your hand into your sleeve and pull out the perfect tool—wah-pow?! Having a multi-function limb like a superhero would be awesome… to a point. It'd also be heavy, and someone would *always* be asking for something.

Sometimes we treat people like they're simply a toolbox of bits and pieces we need or want. We see cool stuff in each person's box of life. We want to take the good stuff and add it to our set of what we have to offer the world: "I'll take her personality and his smarts and her hair, please!" We make this little assumption that if we had bits and pieces of other people, then we'd be more whole, but the opposite is actually true. The more we focus on others, the less complete we feel.

Our faces and rooms would look crazy if we had everything we ever said we wanted. We'd have two noses, three styles of hair, and four sets of sparkling, perfect teeth. We'd all have an embarrassing amount of clothes and shoes pouring out the door. Our room would have decorations and pillows from every store, magazine, Insta-influencer, and website we've ever envied—and I bet it wouldn't even look like the pictures we had admired. And think how many jobs you'd have if you were an Olympian, an actress, a politician, *and* an expert in your field—if you took those tools from someone else's box. Talk about overwhelming.

Finding things we like about each other is fine. Deciding we are less of a person because we don't have those bits and pieces is wrong. And concluding we are more worthy of the good stuff people have than they are—that shows the cavern in our hearts.

I remember encouraging one of my daughters not to be jealous of someone who scored higher than her in a couple of her classes. I said enormously comforting things, like, "I don't want her to be my daughter. I'm so glad you're mine," to which she said candidly, "I don't want to *be* her, Mom. I just want her grades." She had not forgotten how good she had it. She didn't want the girl's struggles, only her grades. Only a little more.

All people, including you, are a complex mix of strengths and weaknesses, good experiences and bad. They are not bits and pieces that can be traded and rearranged like Legos®. Each segment of a person's life is not isolated from the others. Choices, experiences, and circumstances collide against each other to form and shape an irreplaceable human being. Someone's gift of compassion or artistry may stem from a sad place in her life. Someone's excellent grades may come from a place of trying to earn approval from a hard-to-please parent. You can't look at others' gifts as if they are a stand-alone commodity. That's like stealing someone's paycheck after they endorse it. That person is putting in the work of living, of trying to figure out how to develop, how to cope—and you want to step in and take away their best parts without living through their difficult ones.

The reality is, the girl who has the look you want may not have a mom or dad you'd ever want. The guy who has the dad you want may struggle with dyslexia. The friend who doesn't struggle with grades like you do may struggle with her weight. The person who doesn't seem to battle her weight may battle depression. Everyone has good and sad stuff in their lives. When we think of people as bits and pieces, envying all the good bits, it leaves out the very real bad pieces. We conveniently ignore habits and difficulties others deal with. You can't compare others' best qualities and moments to your worst. That's not fair to ourselves. That's not fair to them. That's not even comparison.

The Bible honestly shows all the dark places that bits-and-pieces thinking takes people, but this story may be the ugliest. In 1 Kings 3, two women come to King Solomon for a legal decision. They both recently had baby boys. They lived in the same house and one of the mothers accidentally lay on her baby and smothered him in the night. She placed her dead baby by the other mother and stole her living child. They told their story to Solomon. To make his decision, he employed a test: he said to his assistants, "Cut the live baby in half and give half to each woman." Solomon did not have any intention of killing the baby. He was watching for the response. When the mother of the live baby said, "No, don't kill the baby! Give it to her," Solomon knew who the rightful mother was. The real mother's passion and compassion for her baby's life was so strong, she was willing to give him up so that he could live.

The beautiful effect of love is this: Love would rather the other person have the better stuff, even if it requires personal sacrifice. The real mother would rather her baby live and call her bitter enemy "mother," than die. A horrid effect of jealousy is this: Jealousy doesn't want only the good stuff the other person has; it also doesn't want the other person to have good stuff. In this story, the woman whose son died wanted the other woman's son. If she couldn't have him, she wanted him dead so that the real mother could not have a baby either. In her grief, she wanted to take good and happiness away from anyone she could.

The same God who gave Solomon the ability to figure out who the rightful mother was rightly discerns our hearts, too. Are we jealous, wanting the good stuff that belongs to others? We can develop a character so confident and content that we can enjoy and affirm our friends instead of feeling threatened by them.

And be careful—have you seen the artistic depictions of the false Hindu gods with multiple arms? That's not who we are, ladies. Wanting *more* and going for it with our own two hands is not God's best for us. It shows we don't trust Him to take care of us—we are relying on ourselves alone.

In nature, nothing is identical. Not a single tree, flower, bird, snowflake, or blade of grass is an exact copy of another. Not one person, either. God is not interested in your becoming a carbon copy of another person or a strange combination of you and her. The *only* person He's really concerned about you becoming more like is His Son, Jesus. And His intent in that is not to erase your personhood but to maximize it.

God is the giver of tools. He delights in the gifts He gave you. He wants to use you, without the clutter of other people's bits and pieces piled up around you. Bits and pieces don't make you whole. Only He can make you whole.

THE PROBLEM WITH SOCIAL MEDIA

On social media, people show snapshots of the best moments of their lives. They typically don't talk about moments of rejection and failure. So when you hold your regular ol' day up beside someone's trip to Florida or someone's photo with a boyfriend, you may feel jealous. Who wouldn't? Remember this, though: you can't compare someone's single moment to your entire life. You can't compare someone's outside to your inside. That friend's vacation won't last forever. That boyfriend who is sweet now may hurt her later.

Don't let the mirage of glamorous-looking moments get you down; pay attention to the good God is doing in your life. Ask Him to teach you to be happy for others and to wait for His very best timing in your life. Don't let social media be an idol, consuming too much of your time and holding power over your emotions and decisions. Don't start unnecessary hurtful habits. Ask yourself if time spent on any activity—even keeping up with Instagram—will end up hurting you. Guard your heart.

CHAPTER 4

Weather-Changing Breath

What's better: getting your way or getting closer to God?

The two angels came to Sodom in the evening, and Lot was sitting in the gate of Sodom. When Lot saw them, he rose to meet them...and said, "My lords, please turn aside to your servant's house and spend the night..." They said, "No; we will spend the night in the town square." But he pressed them strongly; so they...entered his house....

But before they lay down, the men of the city, the men of Sodom, both young and old, all the people to the last man, surrounded the house. And they called to Lot, "Where are the men who came to you tonight? Bring them out to us, that we may know them." Lot went out to the men at the entrance, shut the door after him, and said, "I beg you, my brothers, do not act so wickedly. Behold, I have two daughters who have not known any man. Let me bring them out to you, and do to them as you please. Only do nothing to these men, for they have come under the shelter of my roof." But they said... "This fellow came to sojourn, and he has become the judge! Now we will deal worse with you than with them." Then they pressed hard against the man Lot, and drew near to break the door down. But the men reached out their hands and brought Lot into the house with them and shut the door. And they struck with blindness the men who were at the entrance of the house, both small and great, so that they wore themselves out groping for the door.

Then the men said to Lot, "Have you anyone else here? Sons-in-law, sons, daughters, or anyone you have in the city, bring them out of the place. For we are about to destroy this place, because the outcry against its people has become great before the Lord...." So Lot went out and said to his sons-in-law, who were to marry his daughters, "Up! Get out of this place, for the Lord is about to destroy the city." But he seemed to his sons-in-law to be jesting.

As morning dawned, the angels urged Lot, saying, "Up! Take your wife and your two daughters who are here, lest you be swept away in the punishment of the city." But he lingered. So the men seized him and his wife and his two daughters by the hand, the Lord being merciful to him, and they brought him out and set him outside the city. And as they brought them out, one said, "Escape for your life. Do not look back or stop anywhere in the valley. Escape to the hills, lest you be swept away." And Lot said to them, "Oh, no, my lords. Behold, your servant has found favor in your sight, and you have shown me great kindness in saving my life. But I cannot escape to the hills, lest the disaster overtake me and I die. Behold, this city is near enough to flee to, and it is a little one. Let me escape there—is it not a little one?—and my life will be saved!" He said to him, "Behold, I grant you this favor also, that I will not overthrow the city of which you have spoken. Escape there quickly, for I can do nothing till you arrive there." Therefore the name of the city was called Zoar.

The sun had risen on the earth when Lot came to Zoar. Then the Lord rained on Sodom and Gomorrah sulfur and fire from the Lord out of heaven. And he overthrew those cities, and all the valley, and all the inhabitants of the cities, and what grew on the ground. But Lot's wife, behind him, looked back, and she became a pillar of salt.

Genesis 19:1-26

Fine-line, wide-tip, felt, ball-point, highlighter, permanent, every color, bubble letters, block letters, all caps and teeny tiny letters, on folders, binders, homework: doodled hearts and that one name written again and again.

Brad Rice.

Brad Rice.

Brad Rice.

In seventh grade, the only thing I loved more than the band Duran Duran, Willy Wonka's Gobstoppers, and my friends was Brad Rice. Even though I didn't have any classes with him, he was on team 7B with me. I could easily see him across the half-height bookshelf walls of our open-concept school. My eyes found him several times a day. He wore camo. He was tan. He was well-liked. All I wanted was for him to like me back.

I didn't realize it at the time but all that doodling was doing damage to my heart. At the very least, it revealed something that lived there. I was writing what I thought would make me feel valid and happy. I, an inexperienced 12-year-old who was still figuring out how to change a pad, thought I knew what my life needed to be complete.

Poor Brad Rice, I was placing on him a power he did not have—the power for his attention to fill something in my soul. Now I can see it, but then I couldn't. This kid hadn't finished growing, couldn't yet drive a car, and hadn't decided on the kind of character he was going to live out, yet I made him an idol. He's not the only person, achievement, or object I've idolized. God has helped me recognize it faster, but I wonder if I'm giving unearned power to something to make me happy now. We cannot guard our hearts enough.

Think about people you desire to notice you. What person or group have you thought would make you happy?

32

Think about achievements or material possessions you want. You may want those because you've prayed about them and sincerely think they'd be great for you. Or do you want them because you think something about them will push you into a better position?

I liked Brad Rice because he was a cutie. But I also liked him because all my classmates liked him. If he liked me back, then I could be sure of what I wasn't so sure about: that I was special. If he liked me, then everyone else would, too. We look for this kind of validation from people and possessions all the time. We decide that attaining them makes us worthy. That's why popularity is a huge driver for humans. Our brains make this little untrue connection: If we are popular, then we are valid. So we do what we can to force that to happen. No matter what it takes.

A superhero changes the direction of the wind and brings a snowstorm with one breath. Remember Frozone from *The Incredibles*? Like characters in a movie, we try to control our environment for our own advantage. If we ever happen to get what we want, beware the person who tries to take it away.

Genesis 19 is full of lessons about holding people and stuff and status too tightly. It is not easy to read. It might even be considered R-rated. But we have to take a look at what is happening here so we don't repeat painful mistakes. God decided it was time to destroy the city of Sodom because of the evil behaviors going on there. The wrong in that city wasn't casual bullying. And the destruction wasn't without warning. Time and time again, the people of Sodom refused to listen to God and stop the abuse of innocent people.

God talked to Lot's uncle Abraham about the decision, and Abraham begged God not to destroy the city because his nephew Lot lived there. God was kind and sent angels to get Lot and his family out of the city before He burned it.

If you read carefully, you will notice what the townspeople wanted to do to the visiting angels. Gross. You will also notice that Lot offers his pure and beautiful daughters to the sex-crazed mob at his door. This offer shows how entrenched Lot's family was in the culture in which they were living. Lot would rather his daughters be gang-raped than relocate. It is sad that living in this city held so much power over Lot. It's almost like he'd been brainwashed that offering his virgin daughters was normal. It's easy for us to judge, but when we write someone's name all over our folder, or feel bitter that we aren't included in a certain group, or stay upset because we can't have certain clothes or be the star, aren't we letting something hold power over us?

Dramatically, the angels handled the mob—they blinded them, got Lot inside his house, and delivered their message: "The city will be destroyed. Warn anyone connected to your family. Then get out."

The sons-in-law-to-be were likely part of the mob outside. They were so egotistical and self-justified about their sin that they thought Lot was kidding when he told them to flee Sodom. And when it was time to go, Lot hesitated. Wow. After the doorway encounter, he really wants to stay? But the angels grabbed Lot's hands and dragged the family out.

"Run to the mountains!" the angels instructed.

"No, not the mountains. We want to live in a city," Lot whined.

"Fine, run to the nearest city," the angels said, "but *go* and don't look back."

When the sulfur fire storm rained down, Lot's wife looked back. Perhaps she longed for her home, her city, the culture, goods, and conveniences she'd grown accustomed to. Perhaps the behavior of the city didn't bother her. Perhaps she enjoyed being esteemed as a wealthy person, and she didn't want to walk away from all she'd accumulated. Her hometown had become more important to her than the protection and direction of the living God. Ultimately, I think part of her had decided she'd rather not live than to live outside of Sodom. She valued her position more than God's gracious provision. And she became a pillar of salt.

Isn't it scary that we can all get to this place—where something is bigger than God in our heart and mind? We think I'll be "better" with that Brad Rice boy or that Free People jacket. Are you beginning to see what comparison can really do inside? It can latch us onto things that don't have the power we give them. We end up holding so tightly to them that, like Lot's wife, we'd rather die than live without them.

> "See, I have written your name on the
> palms of my hands."
> Isaiah 49:16, NLT

It's time to stop trying to change the weather—time to stop trying to control what everyone thinks of you. Embrace your age, GPA, bank balance, and number on the scale. You can trust God to love you right where you are. God has written your name on His hands, so He's not going to forget you. He sees you, and He alone can provide the assurance, satisfaction, and joy your heart needs.

CHAPTER 5
Jet Pack
Comparison makes us rush.

Now Lot went up out of Zoar and lived in the hills with his two daughters, for he was afraid to live in Zoar. So he lived in a cave with his two daughters. And the firstborn said to the younger, "Our father is old, and there is not a man on earth to come in to us after the manner of all the earth. Come, let us make our father drink wine, and we will lie with him, that we may preserve offspring from our father." So they made their father drink wine that night. And the firstborn went in and lay with her father. He did not know when she lay down or when she arose.

The next day, the firstborn said to the younger, "Behold, I lay last night with my father. Let us make him drink wine tonight also. Then you go in and lie with him, that we may preserve offspring from our father." So they made their father drink wine that night also. And the younger arose and lay with him, and he did not know when she lay down or when she arose. Thus both the daughters of Lot became pregnant by their father. The firstborn bore a son and called his name Moab. He is the father of the Moabites to this day. The younger also bore a son and called his name Ben-ammi. He is the father of the Ammonites to this day.

Genesis 19:30-38

In a movie, a cool super power would be for the hero to be able to fast forward in a time-capsule jet pack past the attacks of her enemy so she'd never get hit. Comparison makes us want to do that, too—strap on a jet pack and zoom past hard times to get what we think we want.

Have you ever approached God like He is the movie producer and you are the writer? You write the script. You choose the ending. You decide the timeline of the story. God provides the resources to make it happen. He is supposed to bow to your plan.

Sometimes human beings stop respecting and trusting God when life doesn't go according to their personal plan. They step completely outside God's will to try to make something they want to happen, happen, bitter that God hasn't already made it happen. Have you ever resisted waiting for God? I have.

Expectations are a form of comparison—maybe not so much comparing our lives with other people, but comparing our lives as they are with how we hoped they would be. When we see that our dreams or plan don't match our reality, we want to rush God. Without realizing it, we try to get around God by manipulating circumstances and people. We hurry things along. Let's pick up on last chapter's story to see how Lot's daughters reacted when their life was suddenly nothing like their expectations.

Remember how Lot argued with the angels about living in Zoar? He wanted his family in a city, not in the country. But the people in Zoar weren't too welcoming, and Lot and his daughters ended up living in the mountains after all. The daughters were probably very sad about losing their home and their mother. Rather than waiting on God or asking for help, they took matters into their own hands when they got restless about their life timeline. They made a conscious decision to get their father drunk and slept with him. I'm sure that's not what they pictured for their wedding night, and I **know** that's not what God planned for them. Their children became powerful people-groups who were violent enemies of their cousins, the Israelites—the Moabites and Ammonites.

Abraham prayed desperate prayers for these two young ladies (Genesis 18:16-33). When God rescued them, they were engaged to be married. Their fiancés acted like God's Word and ways were a joke—not the kind of person you'd enjoy being married to, but Lot's daughters *knew* that's what they wanted. These young women had seen God's angels pull them away from death. But God's deliverance wasn't wondrous to them—it was a let-down. They didn't view it as life-saving and gracious, because they didn't want to leave Sodom. When God rescued them, they ended up living in an undecorated mountain cave with no mother, no boyfriend, and no culture. It wasn't what they wanted. They said there were no men in the whole world, yet their Uncle Abraham and his fine community of talented farmers didn't live too far. They created that excuse. They did what they thought would cure what God "did to" them.

How could these young women fail to trust God? First, they hadn't longed and prayed for rescue at all. They wanted life as they knew it, and God's rescue—though it was the very best thing for them—was, to them, an interruption, not a blessing. God's work in their lives—though it was far from over—was uninvited. Now the daughters were so angry with God for messing up their expectations that they could not and would not wait for Him to open the next door. They strapped on their jet pack and time-traveled to their next expectation, their next dream, without waiting for God.

BEING HEARD

Being heard makes all of us feel loved. When someone hears us, then **acts upon** what was said, it communicates value like nothing else can. When deliverance seems delayed, it feels like we are not heard. God is not acting quickly enough. We want to scream, "Are you even paying attention to me?!" In Psalm 5, David models persistence in prayer. He waited, watched, and expected God to work, even though it took almost 20 years from the time he was anointed king until he actually took the throne. When it doesn't feel like you're being heard, know that you are. Obey God from that place of certainty. Resist giving in to the rebellion your emotions tell you to try.

Like Lot's daughters, I have complained when God said it was time to move and I wanted to stay, or when it seemed He delayed a dream. Like Lot's daughters, I have been so angry with God for how my life turned out that I took decisions into my own hands. I thought I knew how to run my life "better" than God. I don't like to admit it, but sometimes I have definitely wanted my plan, my timing, and my expectations more than God's clock. I have felt that God doesn't care about my dreams, when He is actually providing for what my heart needs most with the interruptions and delays He has allowed.

I have seen again and again that *God's foresight and insight is* **always** *provision and protection.* I want to get to the point where my default is to trust His plan rather than jet-packing to follow my idea of what's next. Jet-packing often gets us in trouble—because we can all make quick, dumb moves when we are angry at life. We can't count how many poor decisions we've made because we think God is throwing a wrench into our expectations.

I know God didn't go to so much trouble to shield these young women from Sodom's vulgar men so that they could throw away their purity soon after. He had a plan for their family and their future. They traded God's idea for their speedier one.

Any of us can get to the place where we're willing to do something vulgar "just one time." Comparison. We look at other people. We should be where they are. We look at our life plan. We should be way "ahead." Our expectations unsettle our hearts and fill us with regret and resentment. We don't see God at work, so we look around for a jet pack to zoom us past the waiting.

Until we get to heaven, we will not fully understand the reasons for the disappointing turns our lives have taken. We can get mad that there have been curves in the road. Or we can see something that Lot's daughters refused to see: the God who rescued us from darkness has a plan. He didn't shield us with His own Son to leave us. We can trust His love.

SAY IT OUT LOUD

The next time Satan tempts you with an inappropriate response to the painful circumstances of life, try saying out loud, "That is NOT a good idea. I do **not** want any part in that. I do **not** want to be that kind of person. Jesus, direct my life. I choose Your ways!"

WHEN PEOPLE DISAPPOINT YOU

Sometimes life doesn't go as planned because of the violations of another person. It is never right for a person to invade you with verbal, mental, physical, or sexual abuse. Talk to a trusted adult right away if this has or is happening to you. Please know that what you experienced is not your fault. It is against the laws of God and society. Abuse happens when sinful, selfish humans choose to disobey God and put their desires above what God teaches. God did not want that pain to happen. He knows how and when it did. He is able to care for the brokenness of your heart as you find safety and heal.

It is normal to feel sad, abandoned, and angry when someone has hurt or shamed you. It is natural to struggle with insecurity and anxiety during and after abuse—not because you are less valuable in any way, but because your identity has been overrun, and that is confusing. It is natural to wonder where God was and why He didn't stop the person. You may feel tempted to look for something that makes you feel immediate relief. Unfortunately, in severe pain, people are often really short-sighted about what will make them feel better. They end up choosing substances, behaviors, or people who add to the wounds of life, rather than healing them.

Please don't strap on the wrong kind of jet pack. Pause. Don't rush to grab temporary happiness. Work with a counselor, talk with Christian friends, and do the work it takes to build a healthy view of God. Release the venom and fear that naturally result from being mistreated.

Lot's daughters thought they were doing what would make them happy, but their decisions hurt generations of people. You do not have to live with a lifetime of regrettable choices. I know life hurts. At times, the pain is agonizing. With God's comfort, you will survive this and use your story and God-given gifts to help others.

Part 2

YOU MAKE ME SICK
What Comparison Is Doing Inside

"We destroy arguments and every lofty opinion raised
against the knowledge of God, and take
every thought captive to obey Christ."
2 Corinthians 10:5

Beginning Thoughts

Sometimes we tease a friend, "You make me sick," when she's lost a few pounds or scored her fifth goal for the night. We mean it as a compliment. Maybe. When we take a deeper look at comparison, though, we often find it is connected to feelings and choices that really are making us sick.

I don't know why, but as we grow up, life often feels like it is more about rejection than acceptance, and we start a steady diet of comparison-based thoughts and decisions. Looks, hair, style, smarts, money, athleticism…if we don't stop ourselves, we get stuck thinking we aren't special in any way because others are "better" than we are in measurable areas like these.

Meteorologists don't know precisely when and where a tornado is going to strike, but they see the weather patterns and warn us. And you can't miss the riddled buildings after it hits. Comparison is like that. We know it is blowing around inside. The thought patterns are familiar. But sometimes we don't realize the damage until after it's been done. In this part, we explore what to do when we start to see comparison's damaging effects.

TAKEAWAYS FOR PART 2

- Toxic thought patterns work like poison, killing our confidence.
- You can learn to recognize destructive thoughts and push them out with Scripture.
- Your value is in your personhood not your productivity.

CHAPTER 6

The If–Then Waves

If you had more, then what?

Now Moses was keeping the flock of his father-in-law...the priest of Midian.... And the angel of the LORD appeared to him in a flame of fire out of the midst of a bush.... And Moses hid his face, for he was afraid to look at God. Then the LORD said, "I have surely seen the affliction of my people...and have heard their cry.... I know their sufferings, and I have come down to deliver them.... Come, I will send you to Pharaoh that you may bring my people, the children of Israel, out of Egypt...."

Then Moses said to God, "If I come to the people of Israel...and they ask me, 'What is his name?' what shall I say to them?" God said to Moses, "I AM WHO I AM....Say this to the people of Israel: 'I AM has sent me to you....'"

But Moses said to the Lord, "Oh, my Lord, I am not eloquent, either in the past or since you have spoken to your servant, but I am slow of speech and of tongue." Then the Lord said to him, "Who has made man's mouth? Who makes him mute, or deaf, or seeing, or blind? Is it not I, the Lord? Now therefore go, and I will be with your mouth and teach you what you shall speak." But he said, "Oh, my Lord, please send someone else." Then the anger of the Lord was kindled against Moses and he said, "Is there not Aaron, your brother, the Levite? I know that he can speak well. Behold, he is coming out to meet you, and when he sees you, he will be glad in his heart. You shall speak to him and put the words in his mouth, and I will be with your mouth and with his mouth and will teach you both what to do."

Exodus 3:1-15, 4:10-15

If I could, I would take all of you to the beach for our Bible study. While we worshipped the Creator oceanside, the waves would join our song. The thing about waves is that they crest, appearing to bring bounty ashore, but then they crush and pull away. Shells become sand. Treasure gets carried away on the ripples of the ocean. And one time, I almost did!

It was the Christmas of my freshman year in high school. My grandpa lived in Puerto Vallarta, Mexico, so we went for a visit. The beach there was gorgeous and I inched my way into the shallow waves along the shore while people called, "¡Blanca! ¡Blanca!" Which means *white*. Which I really, really am, especially in December. So there I was in my stylish 80's swimsuit with my blinding legs, hopping up and down in the waves like a scared chicken, when a huge wave came out of nowhere, knocked me down, and pulled me underwater. It dragged me along the rocky, rough bottom, then down into a cold, deep pocket farther from shore. As I pushed my way out of the water, another wave piled over me, then another. It was probably only about a minute, but it felt like an eternity before I broke free of the waves and caught my breath. I looked down at my pasty legs. Sand was plastered all over me. Mortified, I realized it was also packed in the crotch of my swimsuit—like a full diaper load. I hobbled up the beach to the public bathroom as fast as I could. I felt many eyes staring at me—and heard the crowd chanting *blanca*. I locked the door and tried to shake off as much of my humiliation as possible. A few minutes before, I thought the waves were beautiful. I still do. But for all their beauty, they have destructive force if they're out of control.

For a second, think of your thoughts as waves—the things you dwell on most cause a huge face of water to rise. And have potential to tow you under. Sometimes our comparing thoughts take on a rhythm like waves. They roll in with promise, then rush out leaving little bits of our heart scattered on the shore. They hold us underwater longer than we expect and make us confused and afraid.

Let's try a little exercise. Fill in the blanks below with the first thing that comes to your mind. I know you may not be struggling with all these comparisons, but be honest about what you've felt on the ones that resonate with you.

- If I could _____ (verb) like her...
- If I had her _____ (noun)...
- If he/she would _____ (phrase) ...
- If _____ (person) would accept me...
- If only _____ (circumstance) had not happened in my life...

We are well acquainted with the "if" thoughts that swell in our heads. We let the response of one person or the lack of one goal control our emotions and thought life. It is much harder to fill in the "then" part of the sentence. Then *what?* You'd be happy? Complete? Life would be easier? You'd feel like you were enough? God could use you? Most of us fail to define a specific "then." Although we think our solutions will make life "better," we don't know for sure that they will. So we dwell on all the "ifs" instead—if I had more, was more, or could do more.... Even Moses struggled with this.

I don't know if Moses had another preacher in mind when he told God he couldn't speak well. A real physical human isn't necessary to slip into comparison. We are completely capable of comparing ourselves with a figment of our imagination, who is usually rather perfect. Whatever was going through Moses' mind, he was thoroughly convinced he was unusable. He kept reminding God about his lack of ability. God told Moses—strongly—that He would put the right words in his mouth. Still, this direct promise was not enough for Moses to overcome his feelings of inferiority.

Some scholars think Moses stuttered, or maybe he was embarrassed about a lisp or his Egyptian accent (remember, he was raised by the Egyptian princess). Maybe he had been bullied about his voice. Whatever the reason, Moses was so afraid about his inability that he begged God not to make Him do what He was asking Him to do. At least Moses was polite. He said, "*Please*, Lord, send someone else" (Ex. 4:13). It doesn't matter how polite we are. If we say no to God—even if it seems "humble" to do so—we are still saying no to God.

Moses' brother Aaron became his spokesperson. He was both a help and a hindrance. Aaron had a gift of being an influential public speaker. But he sometimes misused the gift. Aaron led the Israelites into idol worship by forming the golden calf. He also used his chatty gift to participate in gossip about Moses' wife with their sister Miriam. We will never know what might have been different had Moses said a confident, "Yes."

Let's talk about our arguments, what we tell God so we have an excuse not to obey. We're right up there with Moses:

- "I'm not a very good influencer/singer/_____."
- "I can't do that."
- "They don't really need me."
- "If I had more talent, then I would."
- "She can do that so much better."

I argued with God about writing this study. "I don't know nearly as much as _____. I don't have the skills necessary. I have failed You so much in my life, why would You want me representing you? If I had more time/insight/ resources, then I would finish." And, like Moses, "I'm not a public speaker."

The thing is, God's work is about God. Not me. Not you. He can and will use whomever He pleases, whether they are "qualified" or not. We cannot manipulate God or change His power with our if/then arguments. We cannot make deals with Him along this line: "If You make me succeed, then I am willing to be used." Who would get the credit then? God has a strategic purpose in using weak people, well-acquainted with failure. God wants people to see His power so they can know He exists and is working. How exciting that He invites us to be part of that—like a lantern through which His light can shine. God's if/then is, "If you are weak, then I can make you strong" (see 2 Corinthians 12:10), and "If you are less, then people can see more of me" (see John 3:30).

I hope someday I will eagerly wave my hand and squeal every time an opportunity arises: "I am weak—use me!" But first I must break the habit of the if/then waves.

Comparison will always find a reason to stop trying. Then we end up doing nothing, absolutely nothing, for the One who gave us everything.

We always start our "if" thoughts with the dangerous assumption that we have excellent ideas—that every single thing we think will make us happy will indeed make us happy. We assume that our solution will turn out better than what God is allowing in our lives. We are really kind of saying that

God's ideas should change. He should line up with our picture of how things should go. The bottom line is, sometimes we think we are smarter than God.

Perhaps what our minds are searching for with the if/then waves is a trouble-free existence, a world where all is peaceful, productive, and protected. Guess what? We are searching for heaven. We are searching for our Knight on the white horse to rescue us (Revelation 6:2 and 19:11). That is coming, but until then, God does a lot of rescuing through people. Every single day He uses ordinary people like you and me to tell others about His extraordinary love.

Do you remember when the disciples were on the Sea of Galilee and a fierce storm rolled over the sides of the boat (Mark 4:35-40)? The disciples felt like Jesus did not care. He slept while the storm raged. Jesus wasn't sleeping because He didn't care. That is not God's nature. Jesus could relax because He knew God's power and plan.

The if/then waves may be crashing over the walls of your mind, making you feel anxious and incapable. Everyone is weak, limited, and sometimes afraid. In fact, admitting our need for God and our failure is the first step every person must take to come to God. **Weakness doesn't keep us from God. It draws us to Him.**

By His estimation, you are of great significance. You are essential to His strategy to build His kingdom. When Jesus lives inside you, you are a carrier of His Light and Truth. You have a job only you can do. So stop looking at the if/then waves. Instead, look at your Savior. He made you. He's got a plan for you.

AT THE CORE OF OUR NEEDS

Many things in our if/then waves are glimmers of what we really need on the inside. We want a temporary boyfriend, but we need lasting love. We want to be attractive and talented, but we need acceptance and affirmation. We want material things, but we need basic physical provision. We want to be the smartest or best at everything, but we need our skills to be validated and to know we can make a difference. Before we give our self-worth away on the if/then shore, before we compare, we need to examine the core of our desires. What is at the root of them? Ask God to meet the genuine needs of your heart.

CHAPTER 7
An Inaccurate Scale

Only God's scale counts.

When they had finished breakfast, Jesus said to
Simon Peter, "Simon, son of John, do you love me
more than these?" He said to him, "Yes, Lord; you
know that I love you." He said to him, "Feed my
lambs." He said to him a second time, "Simon, son
of John, do you love me?" He said to him, "Yes,
Lord; you know that I love you." He said to him,
"Tend my sheep." He said to him the third time,
"Simon, son of John, do you love me?" Peter was
grieved because he said to him the third time, "Do
you love me?" and he said to him, "Lord, you know
everything; you know that I love you." Jesus said to
him, "Feed my sheep".... And after saying this he
said to him, "Follow me."

Peter turned and saw the disciple whom Jesus
loved. . . . When Peter saw him, he said to Jesus,
"Lord, what about this man?" Jesus said to him, "If
it is my will that he remain until I come, what is
that to you? You follow me!"

John 21:15-22

When my dad and his brother were little boys, they lived next door to a pig farm. One day, they took a lasso and placed it on the ground next to a tree in the middle of the pig pen. They climbed the tree, holding the end of the rope. When a little pig waddled into the lasso, they pulled on the string. The dangling piglet squealed and snorted. Don't worry, their experiment did not last long. The mama pig rushed to the base of the tree and scared them so much, they let the piglet down and ran home. Aren't you relieved to know that little pig didn't swing in the breeze all day?

When we compare, we lasso our own hearts, pulling a cord of doubt and insecurity around them. We let our thoughts swing up, down, and around. That word picture reminds me of the old-fashioned scales that have two cups hanging from a metal rod. A shopkeeper would put the item you were buying—let's say candy—in one cup and a pre-measured weight in the other cup. When the two cups stopped swaying and the rod balanced in the middle, the shopkeeper would know how many ounces of candy you were buying. Of course, you'd want the scale to be accurate. If the owner said you owed her for three pounds of chocolate when the cup held only three ounces, that wouldn't be fair. And if I stood on my scale at home and it read ten pounds heavier than my doctor's office, you can be sure I'd chuck it! We don't like it when scales read wrong (unless, of course, they are in our favor).

God knows people well. From the very beginning, He warned against dishonest scales, because He knew people would try to cheat one another. In Leviticus 19:35-36, He said, "You shall do no wrong in judgment, in measures of length or weight or quantity. You shall have just balances, just weights." God is concerned with *every transaction* in the shopkeeper's store—and in our private lives. He wants integrity. Your mind acts as a scale. God wants honest measures—accurate judgment—in every one of your thoughts, too.

Comparison is the act of weighing something's worth when placed alongside something of similar make up. In the grocery store, you compare the price per ounce. Online, you watch for which site has the best sale on the item you want. But person to person, comparison is like putting yourself on a scale. You hang there, wondering how much you're worth, against something that is really very different from you.

And our scales aren't anywhere near reliable. The scale we use when we compare people to people is off by at least six measures, and all six of these incorrect assumptions could happen within a day.

- You measure yourself too light (not valuable enough).
- You measure yourself too heavy (superior to others).
- You measure other people too heavy.
- You measure other people too light.
- Other people measure you too light.
- Other people measure you too heavy.

By its nature, comparison pits two objects—people—against one another. Do we really want to think and live like that? Here's another problem: comparison's scale swings wildly. It is not based on an absolute measurable standard. We can't even agree with our own personal opinion from one day to the next! A friend may weigh in on the less valuable side one day, but be worth more the next. One woman may be worth a lot to one person's scale and not as much to someone else. When we compare, we can push the balance to our side or away from it, depending on our mood. If we used that kind of scale in business, no one would visit our shop.

Believing comparison's scale is like trusting a random stranger to give you advice on what home or stocks to buy. We would not make a major decision based on a stranger's opinion. We have to trust the source before we sink everything we've ever worked for into an investment. But in our emotional life, we invest ourselves quickly. We easily feel dejected without considering whether someone's opinion of us is accurate, has anything to do with what God says, or stems from a reliable source. We spend a lot of time worrying about people's groundless words, while we neglect God's good, true ones.

One fall, my youngest daughter had outgrown the previous year's sweaters, so I stopped in a couple stores to see what I could find. In one store, I asked the clerk if they had black cardigans. He looked at me as if I were from Mars, swayed his palm to show me the expanse of the store, rolled his eyes, and said with some attitude, "No, we don't. We don't carry black. At all. In anything. We have no. Black. Clothes."

I got the message about the sweater. I got another message, too. He, for whatever reason, was expressing judgment. Any other day, his sneer may have bothered me, but I had been meditating on this day's lesson, so it didn't. The truth is, I asked a question, politely and with a smile. I was interested in shopping in his store and adding to his commission. His out-of-place response to me could have made me feel small, dumb, or embarrassed, but then I would have been trusting a miscalibrated scale. He did not know me **at all.** I did not need to let his opinion of me drain joy from me and cause me to worry about my worth.

Likewise, I resisted the urge to put him on my mind's revengeful scale. God didn't give me life and strength and breath so I could go around judging store clerks I do not know. I understand how tempting that is, but God wants more from us than that. My job is to pray that God will help that clerk and point him to Christ.

Maybe I'll have another encounter with that individual, maybe not. If I do, I don't want to blow a chance to show and tell him about Jesus' love. Every day, we can respond positively or negatively when people attempt to make us feel ashamed for no reason.

We must know and believe we are loved by God. That's the only way we can overcome the everyday struggle to overreact to rejection—and so often we do that by becoming rejecters of others. **We must know grace so we can extend it.**

God's scale, unlike comparison's, compares us to Him alone. On judgment day, God won't put a person beside us and say, "Let's see how you look compared to Sarah. Then I'll decide whether to let you into heaven." On judgment day and today, God compares us only to His holiness. Guess where that puts us on the balance? Daniel 5:27 says it poetically, "You have been weighed in the balance and found deficient."

We have only one hope for having a life that weighs anything on God's scale: **asking Jesus to step on the scale with us,** inviting Him to replace our utter deficiency with the full weight of His goodness and mercy. Because of His compassion, because He removes our sin with His blood, our worth is revealed and our purpose is restored.

When Jesus was on trial before his crucifixion—well, it wasn't much of a trial, rather a crazy, chaotic scene of false accusations—Peter and John stuck around to see what was happening to Him (John 18). During the course of the night, Peter denied that he knew and followed Jesus three times. He even cussed like a country song to try to get people to believe he wasn't part of Jesus's crew. In his betrayal, Peter was seeking the crowd's approval. He feared the kind of rejection Jesus was facing. He wanted what we all do—acceptance, importance, to be popular with the group.

After Jesus rose again, Peter tried to avoid discussing his big mistake with Jesus. He pretended it didn't happen instead of saying a brave, specific apology. (I sometimes want to handle my mistakes that way, too.) Jesus knew Peter was dealing with consequences of the betrayal. Perhaps Peter felt inferior, like he should not tell others about Jesus after he had failed so significantly. That's common. Sometimes we think we can't come to God or do anything for Him because we have messed up. That perpetuates the sin and darkness, rather than resolving it. To neglect the power God has to change our lives does not do anyone any favors. Calling ourselves names doesn't earn us forgiveness. To swing on the scale in the breeze, day after day, wondering if we are worth anything or if He can use us, is to completely ignore Redemption.

Jesus knew Peter needed closure—a public restoration for his public failure. So He asked if Peter loved Him the same number of times he had denied Him. Jesus was helping Peter get over any feelings of being unworthy to work for God. He wanted Peter to take up telling others about Him and nurturing young believers for the rest of his life: "Feed My lambs, shepherd My sheep, feed My sheep." In this beautiful exchange, Jesus wanted to show Peter he was released from condemnation.

But Peter had one more question for Jesus. "What about him?" Peter asked, pointing to John.

Let that sink in. Jesus personalized this exchange to help Peter move forward without shame. Peter cocked his head and spoiled the moment with comparison.

Patient, Jesus taught Peter once more to stop looking around and focus on Him—Who He was, what He was doing in and through Peter. "What is that to you? *You*, follow Me," Jesus answered.

Christ's restoration transformed Peter from approval-seeking to bold, even willing to die for Jesus. He became unafraid of being rejected by humans. We owe the spread of the Gospel to Peter and the other disciples—we may never have heard about Jesus if it weren't for their courage. They collectively worked hard to start the church. They had no time to look from side to side when running that race.

Really, there's not time to look from side to side now, either. Seven billion people live in our world. I don't know how many have heard about Jesus, but I'm certain billions of people still need the gospel message, and believers need discipleship and encouragement. We have too many people to reach to climb on the scale Jesus already settled on the cross.

When you look at yourself on one end of the scale and a talented acquaintance on the other end, you may feel your gifts are very small. God is not looking for heavy gifts. He is looking for people who worship Him in spirit and in truth (John 4:23).

CHAPTER 8

The Parasite of Pride

Pride takes more from you than you meant to give.

In the spring of the year, the time when kings go out to battle, David sent Joab, and his servants with him, and all Israel.... But David remained at Jerusalem.

It happened, late one afternoon, when David arose from his couch and was walking on the roof of the king's house, that he saw from the roof a woman bathing; and the woman was very beautiful. And David...inquired about the woman. And one said, "Is not this Bathsheba, the daughter of Eliam, the wife of Uriah the Hittite?" So David sent messengers and took her, and she came to him, and he lay with her. (Now she had been purifying herself from her uncleanness.) Then she returned to her house. And the woman conceived, and she sent and told David, "I am pregnant."...

In the morning David wrote a letter to Joab and sent it by the hand of Uriah. In the letter he wrote, "Set Uriah in the forefront of the hardest fighting, and then draw back from him, that he may be struck down, and die."...

The messenger said to David, "The men gained an advantage over us and came out against us...but we drove them back.... Then the archers shot at your servants.... Some of the king's servants are dead, and your servant Uriah the Hittite is dead also."...

When the wife of Uriah heard that Uriah her husband was dead, she lamented over her husband. And when the mourning was over, David sent and brought her to his house, and she became his wife and bore him a son. But the thing that David had done displeased the Lord.

2 Samuel 11:1-5, 14-15, 23-27

My dad and his brother had many more adventures than the piglet. They also ran a "club." One day, some neighbor kids who went to a different school came to play. They thought my dad and uncle were the coolest guys ever (they still are). "We want to be in your club," they said, so my dad and uncle came up with a plan.

"You can be in our club. All you have to do is walk through our bucket of gunk," they said, and everyone agreed.

The neighbor kids waited while my dad and uncle ran around the farm and filled the bucket with great stuff like mud and crushed up leaves—no big deal for kids to play in. Then they added some manure. And then some red paint they found in the tool barn. They didn't realize it, but the paint was oil-based and could be scrubbed off only with a strong paint remover like turpentine. They used a big stick to stir the concoction, and the poor neighbors waded in the bucket, no clue what they were stepping into. When they tried to wash off the goo covering their legs, they couldn't get the red paint off. Those kids never came over to play again.

Sometimes we want to belong to the cool kids club so desperately that we step into a bucket of manure and paint without knowing what we are getting into. What makes us willing to abandon common sense and go along with others' ideas? A lot of our peer-dependence stems from wanting to fit in. That's normal and healthy—until our desire to be liked blinds us and we do what our foolish friends tell us to do.

We don't like to see it this way, but comparison often comes from pride. We don't want to call comparison an ego trip, because we are usually feeling bad about ourselves when we are most tempted to compare. If I dig around in my heart at all, though, I see that often comparison stems from a desire to belong to the best group, to be admired. Wanting to fit in or be the best leads to actions that are self-promoting—something as "small" as cheating on your math quiz, or something as "big" as drinking at a party. Unstopped, our behaviors become marked by an excessive concern with personal happiness and a lack of care for what it does to the people around us. Comparison will convince us to try anything once.

Here's what you need to know, though: when you decide to cater to your personal happiness and do not have concern for others, you may step into a nasty bucket. What you choose may bring temporary relief from feeling down, but often ushers in deeper and longer-term pain—more rejection, increased anxiety, and inescapable consequences. Let's take a peek into David's life and see where pride can take us and what it takes *from* us.

Second Samuel 11 tells us the story of David pursuing Bathsheba. At this time, David was about 50 years old. He had been chased by crazy King Saul for almost 20 years but had remained faithful to God and to the king before becoming king himself. He had ruled for a couple of decades now, and he was settled in his palace and commanding his army to go out and defend his nation from enemies. No one in the entire region compared to David in power, prestige, or perhaps even looks. He was, in a way, incomparable. In this high peak of his life, he had a married woman brought to him, asked his attendants and military leaders to look the other way, and manipulated others to have her husband killed in battle. When he had everything, why did he need this one more thing?

Comparison usually doesn't make sense. Even though David may not have compared in the sense that he thought someone was better than him, he may have been comparing the feelings he anticipated having when sleeping with

Bathsheba to his boredom while his troops were away. He should have been with his troops—planning for the protection of his people. Instead, he found something else to entertain him—something which, years later, ended up hurting his kingdom and his family. David had no idea what kind of bucket his pride was prompting him to step into—he simply wanted this pleasure and didn't want to stop himself.

We look for pleasure, too—substances, experiences, food, or a person who will make us feel the significance we have waited years to feel. As humans, we love the tangible, things we can touch, taste, and measure. Things we wait for and believe without seeing are harder to pursue. It is instantly gratifying to have an outfit that is nicer than everyone else's. Even an emotional rush—like David's with Bathsheba—can be a tangible thing. In choosing what will make us feel special, our deciding factor is not lasting satisfaction; it is immediate gratification. In fact, we are often both *shortsighted* (we see only what is right in front of us) and lop-sighted (we think only about the good feelings a choice can give, not the difficult consequences). We don't think where our "happiness" can take us years down the road. We want to be happy now. *Instant* is more important than *healthy*.

The problem with instant is, it goes away. It lasts until the next friend has her shopping spree. Or that guy dumps you. Or the high is gone. Or the boredom returns. Superiority and control are an illusion. Satan's offer of significance, however it is packaged, is always a counterfeit and comes at a price. In the end, his deceit leads to bitterness, misplaced affection, and overattachment to the wrong things.

If you haven't figured it out, Satan's greatest aim is not to make you happy. His goal is to destroy you. Total destruction. Complete immobilization. He loves it when we are disappointed with God. In my own life, he tries to turn my head from seeing God's lasting promises with temporary attractions: "Lookie, lookie! Over here." Choices made in pride promise to fulfill you, but in the end they result in the greatest rejection, humiliation, and even more disappointment.

Recently, I had an ugly rash on the corners of my mouth. The dermatologist said it was because my skin was starting to droop. Oh dear! He prescribed an ointment and told me it would go away quickly, but it didn't. The rash spread. When I returned to the doctor, he told me that the medicine had triggered another problem. The cure made the wound worse. Isn't that what happens? Self-focused cures promise to help us look or feel better, but they end up making our initial problem—our insecurities, our guilt—throb with deeper emptiness. What we choose to fill up the holes in our hearts dig bigger holes. The bucket we step into leaves a stain we can't scrub off.

If you want permanent life satisfaction, you have to find something that will make you truly content and bring you joy and confidence lifelong. Think about it: is there anything this world could offer you that meets this criteria? If you could pick anything—absolutely any person, possession, or situation was within your realm of control and at your disposal—what would you pick that would last permanently, solve more than one problem, and speak to your heart's deepest needs? Is anything better than closeness with God?

You are not longing for a bigger house. For a new car or a stronger body. For perfect health or a great man. I'm not saying these desires aren't real or important, but let's lift our heads to look a little higher. Longer term. What you need most is to know Jesus loves you. To know for certain you are significant, regardless of others' opinions, current circumstances, and fluctuating emotions. What we are waiting for is heaven. What we are looking for is Jesus and His love.

God was gentle with David and helped him realize his need to repent. He is patiently calling us to come closer to Him, too. If we will draw close, I believe we will find Him to be more than enough to satisfy.

THE PROBLEM WITH HAPPINESS

It sounds innocent to pursue happiness, but happiness is often focused primarily on *oneself* and *this moment*. Contentment is different; it focuses on recognizing God's goodness and becoming a more grateful, peaceful person. This is something people can learn with practice. Here are some problems with looking solely for personal happiness:

- The thing (item, person, circumstance, experience, status) cannot make us **permanently** happy. We look for the *next* thing.
- The thing that you think will make you happy is sometimes unattainable.
- The thing that makes you happy lets you down.
- Others get the thing.
- Our idea what will make us happy changes frequently—it is emotion- and impulse-driven rather than chosen with thought and wisdom.
- Our definition of what will make us happy sometimes crosses the line into immorality or becomes unhealthy and even addictive.
- We cannot control people and circumstances to arrange our constant happiness.

Almost always, we assume that our idea of what will make us happy is "better" than what we currently have, and that may not be true.

CHAPTER 9
The Blanket of Shame

You are not who people say you are.

It pleased Darius to set over the kingdom 120 satraps... and over them three high officials, of whom Daniel was one, to whom these satraps should give account, so that the king might suffer no loss. Then this Daniel became distinguished above all the other high officials... because an excellent spirit was in him. And the king planned to set him over the whole kingdom. Then the high officials and the satraps sought to find a ground for complaint against Daniel with regard to the kingdom, but they could find no ground for complaint or any fault, because he was faithful, and no error or fault was found in him. Then these men said, "We shall not find any ground for complaint against this Daniel unless we find it in connection with the law of his God."

Then these high officials and satraps came by agreement to the king and said to him, "O King Darius, live forever! All the high officials of the kingdom...are agreed that the king should establish an ordinance and enforce an injunction, that whoever makes petition to any god or man for thirty days, except to you, O king, shall be cast into the den of lions.... Establish the injunction and sign the document, so that it cannot be changed, according to the law of the Medes and the Persians, which cannot be revoked." Therefore King Darius signed the document....

When Daniel knew that the document had been signed, he went to his house where he had windows in his upper chamber open toward Jerusalem. He got down on his knees three times a day and prayed and gave thanks before his God, as he had done previously. Then these men came...and found Daniel making petition and plea before his God. Then they...said before the king, "Daniel...pays no attention to you, O king,...but makes his petition three times a day."

Then the king, when he heard these words, was much distressed and set his mind to deliver Daniel. And he labored till the sun went down to rescue him. Then these men...said to the king, "Know, O king, that it is a law of the Medes and Persians that no injunction or ordinance that the king establishes can be changed."

Then the king commanded, and Daniel was brought and cast into the den of lions. The king declared to Daniel, "May your God, whom you serve continually, deliver you!" And a stone was brought and laid on the mouth of the den, and the king sealed it with his own signet and with the signet of his lords, that nothing might be changed concerning Daniel. Then the king went to his palace and spent the night fasting; no diversions were brought to him, and sleep fled from him.

Then, at break of day, the king arose and went in haste to the den of lions. As he came near to the den where Daniel was, he cried out in a tone of anguish. The king declared to Daniel, "O Daniel, servant of the living God, has your God, whom you serve continually, been able to deliver you from the lions?" Then Daniel said to the king, "O king, live forever! My God sent his angel and shut the lions' mouths, and they have not harmed me, because I was found blameless before him; and also before you, O king, I have done no harm." Then the king was exceedingly glad, and commanded that Daniel be taken up out of the den. So Daniel was taken up out of the den, and no kind of harm was found on him, because he had trusted in his God.

Daniel 6:1-23

One Christmas, a friend sent my mother-in-law an expensive box of beautiful chocolates. She told us we could each have *one*. We have a big family, and the candy would have been wiped out before they got around the circle if she hadn't made that stipulation. I heard her instructions. But the chocolates were so yummy that even though I was a grown adult, when everyone was out of the room later, I popped the lid open and ate a second. I apologized. My mother-in-law hugged me and giggled at my sweet tooth, but I still remember the guilt. Chocolate gets me every time.

We feel guilty about so many things—sometimes because we cross a line and need to apologize. But sometimes we feel guilt for wrong reasons—an overall general feeling that we should be better or more than we are. Where does this come from? You guessed it: comparison. We feel like we are not good enough, so we look around to see how we are doing measured to other people. Then to feel better, we pick a "remedy" we shouldn't and feel guilty all over again.

FEELING GUILTY?

Circle the areas that burden you, and list others on the lines.

Grades	Weight
Cheating	Stealing
Not being a good person	Lying
Not being able to help a friend	Being late
Wanting more money	Mean words/gossip
Self-centered attitude	Sexual activity
Angry outbursts	Saying no to a friend
Feeling not talented enough	Cussing
Not being smart enough	Reading trashy books
Wrong thoughts	Feeling behind
Watching inappropriate movies	Being sick
Being on your phone too much	Being afraid

_____   _____

In my life, I have felt lots of kinds of guilt—true guilt because I sinned, yes, but also false guilt: shame others wanted me to carry around, and feeling rotten because I wasn't a better person. I struggle with feeling guilty for not being able to give or do more. I'd like to think my heart is so big that I want to be generous and serve well. Sometimes that may be the case. Other times, I want people to think I'm a giver and a doer, so it bothers me when I can't show off more. In that case, my guilt stems from how I look in the eyes of others.

My parents are amazingly organized people. I grew up under that rhythm and respect it fully. But I am messy. My work is creative in nature and requires lots of little supplies that get scattered—and lost. My schedule and my house are full of people, not cleanliness. At times, my brain fights against feeling guilty that I am not more organized. In this case, my guilt stems from upbringing, expectations for myself, and tendency toward perfectionism.

I have friends that run. Miles. I have friends who have more financially than I do. If I am not careful to guard my thoughts, I can easily slip into feeling guilty for not being "as good as" they are. Some of the reasons for my weakness in these areas are due to my own poor choices. But most reasons are not at all within my control—and, if I didn't guard against it, I could feel guilty about those, even though that guilt is not mine to own.

Sometimes I have felt too responsible for friends' feelings, sad when I couldn't erase their pain or do more for them. I imagine you have, too. If this is you, let me say, God loves your tender heart. But concern for others can cross a line. When we constantly feel like we should be able to rescue everyone, or do more than what's healthy to make another person happy, maybe we are overly dependent on helping others as our identity. You are not responsible for the happiness and choices of others. In fact, you cannot control *any* aspect of another person's life. You can choose to be a blessing and to honor God with your kindness, but often all of our effort isn't enough to change people's situations.

I have felt guilty when someone thought I did something that I did not do, when gossipers spread lies and the crowd believed them before asking my side of the story (yes, even in church). Very little in my life has hurt as much as that.

So much guilt...it covers us like a blanket. Instead of pushing it off, we let it stay there smothering us. Here's the thing: guilt isn't a good tool for real life change. Guilt cannot change past mistakes. It cannot change current circumstances or the condition of a human heart. Guilt does not motivate us to change for the right reasons—it only makes us want to change enough to measure up to whomever we are comparing ourselves. Guilt doesn't take weakness away like it promises. It attaches you more concretely to the feelings of weakness. Guilt doesn't communicate clear, constructive action steps. Most of the time, thoughts stemming from false guilt don't even make sense; they are confusing. Daniel shows us a better way to handle guilt: look to God, *not people*, for your identity.

Daniel's co-workers were so jealous of the respect and position the king gave him that they came up with a plan to take him down. They wrote a national law they knew Daniel would not keep: worshipping and praying to the king instead of God. That would be out of the question for this man whose character and faith had distinguished him.

When Daniel got thrown in the lion's den as punishment for praying to God, he did not fight and proclaim his innocence. He knew he was not guilty of disrespecting the king, as his accusers claimed. At around 80 years old, he also knew God could be trusted. So he waited for God to prove Himself, and God did so in a dramatic way—the lions' mouths stayed closed. I wonder whether the big cats all curled up and fell asleep—Daniel with them—or if they were still hungry and frustrated they could not bite. Either way, the deliverance was astounding. Daniel took no credit. He gave attention and praise to God.

Throughout history, people have been accused of all sorts of things they are not guilty of. The apostle Paul was criticized in every way—being too long winded, being too easy on sin, being too harsh, and being too difficult to understand.

TYPES OF GUILT

Inferior guilt—guilty feelings because we don't feel as good as another person or "good enough"

Vague guilt—ashamed feelings about many general things, not traceable to a specific sin

Expectation guilt—disappointment that life did not meet your expectations or that you did not perform your best

Overresponsible guilt—a constant feeling that you disappoint others because you cannot do more to please, appease, or help them

Blame & shame—guilt that others try to say you have although you are innocent

True guilt—feeling sorry that you offended God or hurt people by your actions or attitudes; real conviction of sin

---

Jesus also took the blame for crimes He did not commit. He who was perfect and blameless paid for the sins of humanity for all of time. Slaves were often wrongly accused. Plenty of people throughout history have been unfairly blamed. It may be happening to you right now by a group of jealous, insecure acquaintances or by a boy whom you wouldn't give what he wanted. What people say about you isn't always true, right, or helpful. God certainly does not listen to human opinion to determine whether a person is guilty or not. He sees the heart of each person. He knows what we are guilty of—or not.

What Daniel models for us is to stay focused on God's purpose for our lives rather than changing who we are and what we're doing because we feel a sense of shame.

Look at the list of guilty feelings you circled on page 66. Place a little **checkmark** by items on that list that are not sin but stem from feelings of inferiority or some other untrue source. **Underline** the behaviors that are sins against God, yourself, and others. We can learn to recognize the difference between false and real guilt and how to handle each.

"If we say we have no sin, we deceive ourselves.... If we confess our sins, he is faithful and just to forgive us our sins and to cleanse us from all unrighteousness."
1 John 1:8-9

Make no mistake, if we sin, we are guilty. God's Word isn't a book of suggestions; He has written commands for us to follow. His holy standards are a gift. He cares enough about us to want us to stay away from things that would destroy us. When people break God's laws, even if they do not know Him, they experience consequences and feel the weight of guilt. Don't deny it when the Holy Spirit shows you that you are doing something wrong. The best response you can have to true guilt and conviction of sin is not shame, though. It is repentance. What's the difference?

Shame is holding onto a feeling of deep guilt, turning your focus again and again to the failure, as if your feeling miserable could erase the wrongdoing. It glues you to the past instead of helping you look forward to a better future, making your mistake bigger and more powerful than it should be.

Repentance starts with a deep feeling of regret for the sin you have committed, then turns the focus to God. Honestly and specifically admit your sin to God, state your belief that Jesus paid for that failure on the cross, and then depend on *Him* to forgive your shortcoming and restore your purpose. The focus is His power to forgive.

Guilt tries to smother our vibrant lives with lie-filled accusations: "I'm not this." "I should be that." The Bible shares lots of good news, but perhaps the greatest news of all is that God loved us so much, He provided a way for guilt to be washed away. In times when guilt is real, Jesus is the only legitimate way to deal with our wrongdoing. When guilt is false, you have permission to pinch the corner of it and fling it off for good!

CHAPTER 10
The Mirage of Reputation

Little i's* turn to big lies.

A man named Ananias, with his wife Sapphira, sold a piece of property, and with his wife's knowledge he kept back for himself some of the proceeds and brought only a part of it and laid it at the apostles' feet. But Peter said, "Ananias, why has Satan filled your heart to lie to the Holy Spirit and to keep back for yourself part of the proceeds of the land? While it remained unsold, did it not remain your own? And after it was sold, was it not at your disposal? Why is it that you have contrived this deed in your heart? You have not lied to man but to God." When Ananias heard these words, he fell down and breathed his last. And great fear came upon all who heard of it. The young men rose and wrapped him up and carried him out and buried him.

After an interval of about three hours his wife came in, not knowing what had happened. And Peter said to her, "Tell me whether you sold the land for so much." And she said, "Yes, for so much." But Peter said to her, "How is it that you have agreed together to test the Spirit of the Lord? Behold, the feet of those who have buried your husband are at the door, and they will carry you out." Immediately she fell down at his feet and breathed her last.

Acts 5:1-10

When you ask little kids what they want to be when they grow up, what do they say? I worked at a school for a few years, and they answered things like professional athlete, YouTuber, singer, doctor, and actor. Why do humans seem to answer with huge, famous, and wealthy aspirations? We have this tendency to want to be big in others' eyes—and we go to great lengths to protect that mirage. Even lie.

"Lying? I don't lie," you say. I'm talking about lying to create a mirage around your reputation: exaggerating—either flat-out lying, general bragging, or giving unspoken impressions about your character and accomplishment for the purpose of appearing **bigger & better** or **less guilty**.

I have exaggerated so that people will think better of me than they should. I like when people notice my kind deeds, so if they think I did more than I really did, sometimes I have let that slide. I have made my side of the story sound very innocent when I needed to apologize to a friend. I don't talk much about my areas of struggle. I'm not proud to admit it, but there are definitely moments I paint a mirage of myself in the minds of others. I don't think I'm alone in this. It such a temptation to make sure people think well of us.

LITTLE I'S AND BIG A'S

*Inferiority, intimidation, insecurity, and inadequacy tempt us to make ourselves look stronger, smarter, richer, and better than we feel. We look to attention, achievement, approval, and admiration for validation. But trying to compensate for self-doubt with accomplishment, attractiveness, or arrogance doesn't cure our core questions. Only the words of Jesus can erase the little i's and put the big a's in the right place.

Let's face it: whether we want to admit it or not, we like to be admired—kind of like a statue, carved from precious materials, all blemishes buffed away, people admiring us. But no statues are living. Some are even hollow.

We think our flawless mirage helps our cause. We will do things we don't want to do, give things we don't want to give, and say great things about ourselves we know are not true to gain approval. All of those are, at their core, a form of lying. People eventually see what is going on inside. We are not as sly as we think. Trying to appear perfect can get us into big trouble. It did for Ananias and Sapphira.

After Jesus rose again, He gave His disciples the job of telling people that salvation is found in Him alone. As people believed their message, they formed groups that met for worship, and the faith communities began taking care of each other like family. A man nicknamed Barnabas, which means *encourager*, sold a field and donated the entire amount to help poor people and widows in the church. A few others did the same. Although giving was part of worship, extreme gifts like giving the entire price of a field were not required. Ananias and Sapphira were under no obligation to sell their field. They also were not required to give the full amount to the church when they did sell it. The field was theirs, and they could keep half and give half, or whatever they wanted to do. Where they went wrong was when they made a pact to tell church leaders they were giving the full amount of the price of the field when they weren't. Why did they do that? Maybe they wanted to give the impression that they gave more sacrificially than the rest of the church. They wanted to look good—in their giving and in their living. They wanted to flaunt their big gift and be admired for being generous, but have money left over to buy things that screamed, "Status!" Maybe they hoped that when people looked at them, they'd be impressed.

When God looked at Ananias and Sapphira's hearts, He wasn't impressed. He saw deceit. He saw selfishness and a hardness in their hearts. He saw pride, not humility. When they were confronted with their sin, they collapsed and died under the weight of their sin.

As with other Bible characters we've studied, God gave Ananias and Sapphira a way out of their sin. When the church leaders questioned their story that the offering was the full price, God was giving them a chance to come clean. I don't think God was looking for the handful of dollars they stashed away. He simply wanted honesty. God always, always moves us to recognize the problems in our heart. He leads us to repentance (not performance) when we walk with Him. Had they confessed their wrongdoing, the outcome for Ananias and Sapphira would have been restoration to God and His Church. But Ananias and Sapphira made their choice. They wanted to look good more than they wanted to do right. Maybe they thought repentance would be humiliating.

Ananias and Sapphira reaped the consequence of their pride, and so did King Hezekiah. In 2 Kings 18, we see how this king of Judah came into his reign with the desire to please God. He tore down altars that belonged to false gods and tried to lead the people well. Then he got so sick, he was at the point of death. He prayed and God gave him a sign that he would be healed by moving the shadows on his steps backwards (2 Kings 20). Hezekiah recognized that God was the source of time and of his very breath.

But, soon after, a neighboring royal family came to visit. They'd heard he was sick. Instead of saying a simple thank you for the fruit basket they brought, he showed off his palace, storehouses, and everything he owned. Isaiah the prophet told Hezekiah that because of his boastful attitude, eventually these neighbors would seize everything he had shown them. Sadly, Hezekiah didn't show regret. Though Hezekiah saw God's astounding, healing work, the wealth he accumulated deceived him into thinking he had premium value.

In Numbers 12, we learn how Miriam and Aaron boasted about their positions as leaders of God's people and their boasting led them to ridicule Moses' wife. David, too, sinned with boasting. After a lifetime of relying on God, he counted his troops, which God had asked him not to do (2 Samuel 24). So it would be foolish if we thought we were immune from wanting others to admire us. Of course we want to be liked. But it may come at a cost.

It is more important to be honest than impressive. Actually, people can relate to you and trust you much more if you admit your faults, apologize, and relax about being so perfect. Say what you need to say (even before someone brings up your mistake to you!): *I misled you. I was selfish. I overexaggerated. I need help. I treated you wrong. I made myself look good, and I lied doing it. I am sorry. Will you forgive me?* God is not afraid of our honesty, so we should not be afraid to be honest, either. In fact, real confession is the pathway to life change. Surprisingly, you'll make a lot of friends that way, too.

We have a choice about how to deal with our need for validation—putting up the façade that comparison tells us we must, or building bridges with honesty. On a desert road, a mirage fades when people get close to it. But you, go ahead and let people get close and see who you really are— your authentic self, not some shined-up version of who you think people want you to be. Show others what Jesus is capable of doing with one life.

HOW TO SAY I'M SORRY

When you make a mistake, an important part of moving forward is making a **sincere** and **specific** apology.

1. Start by saying, "I know I messed up."
2. Then say what you did wrong—without making excuses or making the issue smaller than it was.
3. Offer compensation if you broke or lost something that belonged to the person.
4. End by saying, "Will you forgive me?"

Listen to the point of view of your friend or family member without the fear of rejection. When you sincerely value a relationship, you learn to do the work to keep it. Just because you mess up doesn't mean you're not a blessing. And if you need to apologize, that doesn't mean you aren't valuable. You are human, and you are loved by God! Knowing this, you can say a sincere, "I am sorry."

Part 3

WHO'S THE REAL HERO?

How Jesus Sets Us Free from Comparison

"God cancel[ed] the record of debt that stood against us
with its legal demands. This he set aside,
nailing it to the cross."
Colossians 2:13-14

Beginning Thoughts

The past few years, Christian speakers and singers have emphasized what God says about us: He calls us His child (John 1:12; Romans 8:14), His friend (John 15:15), forgiven (1 John 1:9), gifted (1 Corinthians 7:7; 1 Peter 4:10), and valuable (Luke 12:24). These promises are true, and knowing our identity in Christ helps us live free from comparison.

But in our search for assurance, I fear we have focused too much on ourselves and too little on our Creator, the One who decided and defines our worth. Without recognizing who God is, we cannot get all excited about who He says we are. Without knowing God's divine place in the universe, hearing all the good things He says about us doesn't change our identity struggle long-term. It's only getting pumped up on flattery. If we don't believe His authority, His saying we're loved is no different than our neighbor or friend saying it. And isn't it kind of self-centered to want to hear that what He says about *our* worth without believing *His*?

Until we understand who God is and what Jesus lived and died to do, we don't really understand where to park our sin and shame once and for all. And until we do that, we cannot navigate others' opinions **or** control our thoughts about ourselves. So before looking at all the things God's Word says about us, let's hear what He says about Himself.

TAKEAWAYS FOR PART 3

- Believing God's uniqueness and authority is the first and most important step to overcoming comparison.
- Believing who God is allows you to stop worrying about who others think you are.
- Knowing Jesus and experiencing His forgiveness helps us know, forgive, accept, and enjoy ourselves.

CHAPTER 11

The Only God

No one compares to God.

When Ahab saw Elijah, Ahab said to him, "Is it you, you troubler of Israel?" And he answered, "I have not troubled Israel, but you have, and your father's house, because you have abandoned the commandments of the Lord and followed the Baals. Now therefore send and gather all Israel to me at Mount Carmel, and the 450 prophets of Baal and the 400 prophets of Asherah, who eat at Jezebel's table."

So Ahab sent to all the people of Israel and gathered the prophets together at Mount Carmel. And Elijah came near to all the people and said, "How long will you go limping between two different opinions? If the Lord is God, follow him; but if Baal, then follow him." And the people did not answer him a word. Then Elijah said to the people, "I, even I only, am left a prophet of the Lord, but Baal's prophets are 450 men. Let two bulls be given to us, and let them choose one bull for themselves and cut it in pieces and lay it on the wood, but put no fire to it. And I will prepare the other bull and lay it on the wood and put no fire to it. And you call upon the name of your god, and I will call upon the name of the Lord, and the God who answers by fire, he is God...." The prophets of Baal...called upon the name of Baal from morning until noon, saying, "O Baal, answer us!" But there was no voice, and no one answered. And they limped around the altar that they had made. And at noon Elijah mocked them, saying, "Cry aloud, for he is a god. Either he is musing, or he is relieving himself, or he is on a journey, or perhaps he is asleep and must be awakened." And they cried aloud and cut themselves after their custom with swords and lances, until the blood gushed out upon them. And as midday passed, they raved on...but there was no voice. No one answered; no one paid attention.

Then Elijah said to all the people, "Come near to me." And all the people came near to him. And he repaired the altar of the Lord that had been thrown down.... And he made a trench about the altar.... And he put the wood in order and cut the bull in pieces and laid it on the wood. And he said, "Fill four jars with water and pour it on the burnt offering and on the wood." And he said, "Do it a second time." And they did it a second time. And he said, "Do it a third time." And they did it a third time. And the water ran around the altar and filled the trench also with water....

Elijah the prophet came near and said, "O Lord, God of Abraham, Isaac, and Israel, let it be known this day that you are God in Israel.... Answer me, that this people may know that you, O Lord, are God, and that you have turned their hearts back." Then the fire of the Lord fell and consumed the burnt offering and the wood and the stones and the dust, and licked up the water that was in the trench. And when all the people saw it, they fell on their faces and said, "The Lord, he is God; the Lord, he is God."

1 Kings 18:17-39

My tiny childhood church didn't have a super-active youth group, so my mom found a Christian camp in the area to give my brother and me some encouragement. As a rising high school sophomore, I thought camp was the best thing that had ever happened to me. Cute boys were *everywhere*. I immediately got a crush on a tall, curly-headed boy named Nathan and talked to him a lot that week. I also noticed a smiley boy named Danny and enjoyed talking to him when Nathan wasn't around. On the last day, both of them told me they liked me. What did I do? I gave Nathan a kiss and told him I loved him. As soon as his church bus pulled away, I gave Danny a kiss and told him I loved him. I wrote them both letters, remained friends with Nathan, called Danny my boyfriend, then met another crush at my cousin's house across the state line and kissed him too. When I told Danny, he broke up with me. I gave his class ring back, and I never heard from him again. I was heartbroken. If he liked me, why couldn't he forgive me?

> "May they know that you alone—whose name is the LORD—are the Most High over the whole earth."
> Psalm 83:18, HCSB

No one wants to be loved with a divided heart. But a lot of people try to do that when it comes to God. Some people claim they do not believe any god or spiritual ruler exists, yet human opinion, addiction, or *something* rules them. On the other end of the spectrum, people around the world believe multiple gods, goddesses, and rituals have power. Some false religions use God's name but teach things that directly oppose the Bible. Some people say they love Jesus but ignore His words and live like they want. No wonder the world is confused about God! Is one spiritual ruler more legitimate than the others? If someone is really sincere and good, will they go to heaven? Is it unfair that the God of the Bible claims He is the only God? What does belief in God have to do with comparison, and why are we talking about it here?

Well, if God is not different from us in His holiness and authority, it does not matter what He says. What I mean is, if He is not the *true* God, then He does not have the right to say, "Your sins are forgiven," or "I made you," or "I love you where you are right now." If His words don't have power, throwing around inspiring phrases about how special He thinks we are is wasted time. They would be empty sayings. But God *is* the true God. Because of His position, we can be certain that His Words about our value and place are true. In this chapter and the next, we will look at distinctions that help us get to know God's rightful place.

> "Before the mountains were born, before You gave birth to the earth and the world, from eternity to eternity, You are God."
> Psalm 90:2 (HCSB)

He Is the Only One

One of the first things God revealed about Himself was that He is the only all-powerful, all-knowing, present-everywhere Spiritual Being. Respecting His unique place is the first commandment: "You shall have no other gods before me" (Exodus 20:3). And He instructed His people to teach this truth clearly from one generation to the next: "Hear, O Israel: The Lord our God, the Lord is one. You shall love the Lord your God with all your heart and with all your soul and with all your might. And these words that I command you today shall be on your heart. You shall teach them diligently to your children" (Deuteronomy 6:4-7).

Some aspects about God are hard to understand. This is because He is different from us. We are humans with limited lifespans and minds. The God of the Bible has always existed (Genesis 1:1-3; Exodus 3:13-15). He is the only thing that was never created. He exists in three persons but is the only God:

1. The almighty Father God, often called Jehovah or LORD (1 Corinthians 8:6), who loves humanity;

2. The Son Jesus, our Salvation, who became God wrapped in human flesh, gave His life to save people from sin (Matthew 16:13-17); and

3. The Holy Spirit, also called the Counselor, who convicts of sin and lives inside believers to comfort and direct them (John 14:26).

God is not required to prove or explain Himself, but He is kind and helps people see Him. He regularly reveals His character and power through His work in the world, like He did in 1 Kings 18. King Ahab of Israel was furious with God's prophet Elijah. The country of Israel had been suffering a drought for three years as a punishment for worshipping false gods, especially two named Baal and Asherah. God's prophets, including Elijah, told King Ahab the reason for the drought. Instead of listening to the prophets, the king blamed them for the drought and killed many of them. The king and queen kept hundreds of "teachers" who promoted Baal and Asherah on their payroll—they ate at their table and misled all the people. So when Elijah came to him with a proposal to have a competition of the gods, Ahab was thirsty to win. Can you picture the tension in the crowd that gathered on the mountain? One man dared to tell the entire nation their view of God was wrong.

The people who followed Baal built an altar, chanted and danced, even cut themselves. But nothing happened. No fire came to burn the sacrifice. No rain came to stop the drought, even though Baal was considered the "god of the storm." Baal was a figment of their imagination. As much effort as the people put into believing this god, he had no power. Their belief system did not advance their lives; it destroyed them.

Then Elijah rebuilt the altar of God and had the king's men waterlog it. Elijah prayed. God licked the hilltop clean with fire in an instant. God showed He was the exclusive and supreme God. The people repented, and rain rushed in. Even though the people had ignored God, He was merciful.

Some people say that all religions lead to the same place, any god will do—they all help people be "good." But they can't all be correct. Each belief system gives a different remedy for sin, a different view of how to live, a different definition for right and wrong, and a different Spiritual Being they hold up as the strongest. Only One God speaks truth and has real, lasting power over all of Creation.

> "Your way, O God, is holy. What god is
> great like our God?"
> Psalm 77:13

Some people say God is restrictive by requiring human beings to believe that He is the Only God. But wouldn't it rather be unkind for Him to let people believe that any god will do when no other Spiritual Being has the position He has? It was understandable—even honorable—that Danny wanted singular devotion. A mother is not mean if she doesn't want her child to call a random stranger, "Mommy." A boss has the right to forbid his workers from telling competitors about their new products, patents, and security passcodes. These expectations are not unreasonable. Parents and corporations have a legal claim to exclusivity. So does God. But if He asks for it, people accuse Him of being narrow-minded.

When we decide that all religions and philosophies teach life lessons of equal value, we are stealing God's identity. We wouldn't be okay with someone using our credit card or stealing our car. It's not theirs. They didn't earn it. We also need to care when people misrepresent God and try to steal His glory by saying He's like every other god when He's not. Only He has earned the title of Almighty God.

From cover to cover, the Bible makes it clear that God is indeed the only Holy Father. It is time to say He is the most worthy One.

I THOUGHT GOD WAS LOVING

Some people say God is unloving because He teaches against other gods or behaviors they want to pursue. This is a misinterpretation of love. Love is *not* saying that everything a person wants to try is okay. Not every behavior out there is healthy. Not every belief system is true.

It would actually be **unloving** for God to passively overlook counterfeits of His work, when they lead to fractured hearts and eternal condemnation. He cannot approve religions, rituals, habits, activities, and addictions that destroy lives—especially those that attach His name to something shameful. That does not mean He lacks love for humans. Instead, we lack respect for Him.

Being afraid to set limits, sound warnings, and share truth is cowardice, not love. God is not a coward. He is powerfully true, and He is passionate about the people He made. It is not unloving that He calls out sin and calls us to holiness; it leads to *life*. It is more than fair that He requires us to admit that He is the only way to eternal life; it is *grace*.

CHAPTER 12
God Is Right
You need God's authority more than you realize.

And Samuel said to Saul, "...Listen to the words of the Lord..., "Now go and strike Amalek and devote to destruction all that they have...."

But Saul and the people spared Agag and the best of the sheep and of the oxen and of the fattened calves and the lambs, and all that was good, and would not utterly destroy them....

The word of the Lord came to Samuel: "I regret that I have made Saul king, for he has turned back from following me and has not performed my commandments." ...And Samuel came to Saul, and Saul said to him, "...I have performed the commandment of the Lord." And Samuel said, "What then is this bleating of the sheep in my ears and the lowing of the oxen that I hear?"...

And Saul said to Samuel, "I have obeyed the voice of the Lord....I have brought Agag the king of Amalek, and I have devoted the Amalekites to destruction. But the people took of the spoil, sheep and oxen, the best of the things devoted to destruction, to sacrifice to the Lord your God in Gilgal." And Samuel said, "Has the Lord as great delight in burnt offerings and sacrifices, as in obeying the voice of the Lord? Behold, to obey is better than sacrifice.... For rebellion is as the sin of divination, and presumption is as iniquity and idolatry. Because you have rejected the word of the Lord, he has also rejected you from being king."

1 Samuel 15:1, 3, 9-14, 20-23

I have friends who say they don't care that the Bible teaches that some things are right and some are wrong. They think God does not have the right to tell humans how to live. You may never have realized what a protection it is to the human race that God teaches against evil and owns the right to forgive sin. These attributes of God—His righteousness and authority—are inseparable from our wholeness as human beings. If He did not speak with the intent to prevent sin and if He could not forgive sin, we'd be in a bigger mess than we already are.

He Is Righteous

When I was 5 years old—old enough to know that money bought candy—my parents kept a coffee mug filled with coins in one of our upper kitchen cabinets. One day, I pulled a chair over, climbed up, filled my palm with coins, climbed down, and put the chair back. Then I went over to the kitchen drawer where my mom kept pencils and erasers—that big gummy kind for art projects. I opened the drawer, took an eraser out, and started rubbing it on my forehead. I was cute and little and that was weird, I guess. But I knew what I was trying to do—wipe away my sin.

Why does sin bother us? Because it hurts! Whether we want to admit it or not, or live by it or not, *rightness* is important to every person. We hate when people take advantage of us. We are furious when bullies hurt others or those in power are corrupt. We would think someone was insane if she said about a child trafficker, "Oh, that's fine. He's entitled to do what makes him happy." Everyone agrees: some things should **never** be done to any human—robbery, rape, torture, oppression.

We may excuse sinful behaviors if we ourselves want to do them: "It's not *that* bad." We may ignore others' misdeeds if they don't directly impact us: "They're not hurting anyone." But when someone directly violates us, or when their misconduct is extreme and public, we stand up and shout that something is wrong. We don't want evil to touch our family or community. Rightness (righteousness, holiness) suddenly matters. Even people who have committed horrific crimes against humanity want to be treated well in prison. They will demand it. How ironic.

Our sense of justice reveals a truth that some people don't want to admit: we were made in the image of a holy and righteous God. In the Old Testament, God reveals His holiness and asks His people to show they belong to Him by living set-apart, pure lives (Leviticus 11:45, 19:2, 20:26; Deuteronomy 23:14). They weren't perfect, though. So they made sacrifices to show their sorrow for their wrongdoing. In the New Testament, God ushered in true righteousness through Jesus Christ and made a way for sin to be permanently cleansed.

> "For the LORD is righteous."
> Psalm 11:7a

One thing that clouds our understanding of God's holiness is that our interpretation of "rightness" revolves around our line, not God's. We don't like His definition of sin, so we make up our own. We make excuses to do the things we want and then wonder why life gets complicated. Another thing that clouds our understanding of God's righteousness is the reality of death and decay. We wonder why God doesn't prevent the pain of loss and mistreatment. It is true that God is sovereign over all that happens. Yet we can't leave out the reality that God never wanted natural disasters, disease, injustice, and abuse. People chose, invited, and participate in the curse by rebelling against God's ways.

Without realizing it, what we ultimately want is for people to act how God teaches them to. We want the world to be like it was supposed to be before sin. We want everything to be right. But *right* starts with a *recognition* that some things are sin and should not be done. God was right about sin all along.

He Is the Authority

The human view of God's authority ranges from complete rejection to full acceptance. Most people think they can park somewhere in the middle. They think they can say that they love Jesus and mean it, but also live like they want. There is plenty in God's Word that people don't like to swallow. If we start picking and choosing what parts of the Bible we like and therefore follow, where does the picking and choosing end?

We really can't say that the Bible is a useful, good book if we think parts of it are useless. Because of its exclusive claims, God's Word is either all true or not true at all. God either has all authority, or He has none. He is either telling the truth, or He is lying. The moment we say we can't trust His guidance about something, then we are saying He is not all-wise. He is not God. And if He is not God, His Word is not credible and there is no reason to follow *anything* the Bible says; no one would need to. But do we really want the Bible removed from all of human experience?

No one really wants a standardless society, and no one wants a standardless God. Picture what that would look like. With our love of sin and self, the human race could literally end within one generation. Yet we insist that we know better than God. We can do what we want. God doesn't understand what He is asking of us, so we shouldn't have to submit to His leadership, whether it is financial, sexual, or another area. And no human should confront us about our choices, either. Maybe the real reason we hate being challenged to consider a different way is because we don't want to hear that Someone has more authority than we do.

King Saul didn't want to hear that, either. Scripture records three times that he rashly insisted on his way rather than God's.

- In 1 Samuel 13, he rushed to offer the sacrifice when only the priest was supposed to do that. He said he wanted to ask for God's help as fast as possible. His "spiritual" excuse didn't make up for disobedience.
- In 1 Samuel 14, he made his whole army join him in going without food until they were victorious, but God did not tell him to lead his troops to fast on a day of battle. It was a misplaced sacrifice.
- In 1 Samuel 15, he partially obeyed God but excused a *little* disobedience.

Let's take a closer look at this last situation. Before going out to battle, God gave Saul clear instructions about completely defeating the Amalekites. That may look callous on the surface, but the Amalekites were a civilization that ravaged others. To let them continue would have been detrimental to others.

Saul understood the danger of this cruel civilization enough to annihilate them without hesitation. But he stopped short of complete obedience. He kept alive the enemy king and the best sheep and cows. Later he said it was for gift to

God, a sacrifice. Then later he said it was because the people demanded it. Sounds like a politician's excuses to me. If he wanted the healthy herds and an enemy king for a trophy, he could simply admit it. Instead, he excused it.

When Samuel confronted Saul for his failure to do what God instructed, Saul said over and over that he had done what God asked. He was completely convinced what he had done was enough. He did not view his actions as rebellious. In the end, God could not tolerate Saul's leadership of his own heart. He took the line of kingship from Saul's family permanently and gave it to David's family instead.

You and I act like this. When it comes to letting God lead, we say we agree with God, but we hold out personal control when we are afraid we will be embarrassed or have to give up personal gain or pleasure. And we are completely convinced we are still following God.

"For my thoughts are not your thoughts, neither are your ways my ways," declares the Lord. "As the heavens are higher than the earth, so are my ways higher than your ways and my thoughts than your thoughts."
Isaiah 55:8-9

Every minute of every day, something or someone is your authority. If you want that authority to be yourself, you can try. You can assert your freedom to put your pleasure or pride before the advice and instructions of a Holy God. Free will is a gift of His grace to us—giving us the option to choose relationship with Him without being forced. If you want to use your free will to resist His authority and be your own, He typically doesn't put a physical stop to that. But there's one thing we are not free from—the consequences of our sin.

One of the consequences of rejecting God's righteousness and authority is being trapped in comparison. When we are the authority, the judge of who is good enough, it is no longer Jesus declaring our worth and value based on His unchanging decision to lay down His life for us. It is now we humans who decide worth and value, along with what is right and wrong. Yikes!

"For the entire fullness of God's nature dwells bodily in Christ, and you have been filled by Him, who is the head over every ruler and authority."
Colossians 2:9-10 (HCSB)

Thankfully, Jesus says, "All authority in heaven and on earth has been given to me" (Matthew 28:18). His rightful place is Ruler over everything. From setting the stars in the night sky to covering our sin, He is on the throne. We don't have to be afraid of God's sovereignty. It is a gift and a very good thing.

CHAPTER 13
Why Jesus Lived and Died

He lived and died for you.

And the soldiers led him away inside the palace.... And they clothed him in a purple cloak, and twisting together a crown of thorns, they put it on him. And they began to salute him, "Hail, King of the Jews!" And they were striking his head with a reed and spitting on him and kneeling down in homage to him. And when they had mocked him, they stripped him of the purple cloak and put his own clothes on him. And they led him out to crucify him....

It was the third hour when they crucified him. And the inscription of the charge against him read, "The King of the Jews." And with him they crucified two robbers, one on his right and one on his left. And those who passed by derided him, wagging their heads and saying, "Aha! You who would destroy the temple and rebuild it in three days, save yourself, and come down from the cross!" So also the chief priests with the scribes mocked him to one another, saying, "He saved others; he cannot save himself. Let the Christ, the King of Israel, come down now from the cross that we may see and believe."

And when the sixth hour had come, there was darkness over the whole land until the ninth hour.... And Jesus uttered a loud cry and breathed his last. And the curtain of the temple was torn in two, from top to bottom. And when the centurion, who stood facing him, saw that in this way he breathed his last, he said, "Truly this man was the Son of God!"

Mark 15:16-20, 25-33; 37-39

My father-in-law Jerrell has been a pastor for more than 60 years. He now leads the church he grew up in as a boy. The church met for decades before constructing a new church building when Jerrell was 12 years old. His father Thomas was instrumental in making sure it was well-built. A few days before the opening Sunday, Thomas took Jerrell with him to do a final check. He climbed a ladder to check something in the attic, and Jerrell asked if he could come up with him. Thomas agreed hesitantly and told him to be careful on the ladder. Jerrell climbed into the attic, but, not used to walking on rafters like his dad was, his foot slipped and plunged through the brand-new ceiling tile in the area above the pulpit. Embarrassed and afraid, he wiggled his foot out, climbed down the ladder, and nervously waited to tell his dad what he had done. When he did, Thomas didn't yell. He didn't accuse Jerrell of clumsiness or tear him down. He had invested months of work and money into the building. Still, he didn't complain, "Why did you have to follow me up there?" He also didn't leave the tile hanging loose—it had to be repaired. Thomas patted Jerrell's shoulder and said, "Don't worry. I'll fix it." He rummaged through his tools, repositioned the tile, and tacked it into place as if it had never happened.

All of us, no matter how sincerely we desire to be good people, have slipped on a rafter of selfishness or impatience. We've plunged through the ceiling tile of someone else's heart with our words, attitudes, and gossip. Even with our best efforts and apologies, we don't have the tools to repair the damage we have caused—and others can't completely fix what they've done to us, either. We need a loving Intercessor to repair what sin has broken without barking belittling words of condemnation. That's what Jesus lived and died to do.

At Jesus' crucifixion, as at all Roman executions, a centurion was in charge of torturing and supervising Him for the duration. The centurion did his job. He may have even felt noble torturing those who were sent to the crosses—they were the worst of humanity: murderers and robbers. He was protecting others. But when Jesus exhaled His last breath, the centurion declared, "Truly this man was the Son of God." Why, after years of military service and hours of mocking Jesus, did he suddenly say out loud, "Truly this man was the Son of God!"?

We know that when Jesus died, the curtain in the temple tore in two from top to bottom—the story is in our Bible. But this man didn't know that had happened. We know that when Jesus died, He opened the way for people to be saved—completely set free from their sin and shame. But the centurion didn't understand all of that. He saw only what was in front of him: the jeering crowd; the proud Roman government officials and the jealous Jewish leaders; the other two men being crucified still feebly trying to catch a breath; and the frighteningly dark sky. The weather is not what changed the centurion's mind.

What changed his mind was seeing Jesus face to face. Something in Jesus' countenance, His Words, and His final breath compelled the warrior to confess what the duties of his job and the jeers of the mob made him resistant to consider: Jesus was no ordinary human. The centurion knew without a doubt that Jesus was divine and different. He was God.

Jesus Is God

The title Son of God reminds us that Jesus' life didn't begin when the angel announced to Mary that she would become pregnant. Jesus is God, who existed before Creation, then put on the body of a human being. The incarnation is astounding and hard to grasp—the reality that Almighty God wrapped Himself in flesh and lived among us. But it is crucial that we acknowledge Jesus is God, and that everything was made by Him (John 1:1-3; 1 Corinthians 8:6; Colossians 1:16; Hebrews 11:3). Without believing this, we cannot be saved. And without that designation, His death would not have power. He'd only be a historical figure dying a tragic, meaningless death. Since Jesus was God, and since He came alive again after He died, He has the ability and right to deliver us from sin's curse. He died to remove our death sentence, and His resurrection gives Him the position of Rescuer.

> "These are written so that you may believe that Jesus is the Christ, the Son of God, and that by believing you may have life in his name."
> John 20:31

Jesus Is Messiah

The Hebrew word *messiah* means "promised and anointed deliverer." Even before sin and decay entered the world, God had a plan to provide for the forgiveness of sin with the life of His Son. Through prophets, God began to make promises about the special Savior who would set people free. How Jesus was born, lived, died, and rose again—every aspect of His life—perfectly fulfilled the prophecies told about Him hundreds of years before He lived. The woman at the Samaritan well was one of the few people to whom Jesus directly revealed He was the Messiah (John 4:25-26), but others recognized His greatness (John 11:25-27). If Jesus said He was the Messiah but He was really not, we cannot call Him a good teacher—He'd be a liar. But since He *is* the Messiah, that means when He came to earth, He knew He was coming to lay down His life for sinners. His passion and purpose was your soul—your redemption, wholeness, and second chance, and mine, too.

Jesus Is Life

We look for lots of things to give us the feeling of being alive. We look for meaning in accomplishments, material possessions, and attention from people. But we are mistaken to think that any person, award, or item can make what's wounded and dead in us alive again. Only Jesus can do that. He said, "I am the way, and the truth, and the life. No one comes to the Father except through me" (John 14:6). Jesus' statement that He was life wasn't lighthearted, like, "Here's one of your many options in a sea of philosophies." He was urging people to see that He was the *only* way to be set free.

"Whoever has the Son has life; whoever does not have the Son of God does not have life."
1 John 5:12

Some people say that Jesus was just a good teacher, but He is so much more than a good teacher. God's Word describes the nature and uniqueness of Jesus Christ. John 21:25 tells us that if everything Jesus did was recorded, the world could not hold all the books written about His works. Although we cannot begin to describe His personhood and love, it's easy to see that He alone is able to fix what our sin has broken. Like the centurion, it is time for us to decide His place in our lives. See Him face to face by spending time in His presence. Read His Word and declare with me, "You are the Son of God."

WHAT HAPPENS WHEN WE DIE?

Pop culture grapples with death by saying that people become angels or stars when they die. Movies say that people we love are "watching over us" and if you're good, you'll go to heaven. People try to comfort themselves in loss, but the Bible is clear: when we die, we do not become angels, stars, or gods.

The Bible says when our bodies die, our souls—the core of who we are—live forever. Live where is the question. Without believing in the one true God and calling on Jesus Christ for salvation, no person, no matter how good, can experience eternal life (John 14:6). When believers die, the soul of the person joins the presence of Jesus in heaven, because their sins have been cleansed by His blood (2 Corinthians 5:8). When unbelievers die, they spend eternity in hell because they are under the condemnation of their own sin (Revelation 20:15). If God allowed sinful people into heaven—people who always did life the way they wanted—then His home would become polluted. For eternity, people would mistreat one another with the actions they never recognized were hurtful during their lives. Heaven would be no different from earth.

Contrary to our culture's false theology, we can't earn our way to heaven. Exactly how good would you have to be? No amount of good can erase selfishness, lying, and other sins. Good is what we are made to do—we don't get bonus points for it. It doesn't earn us a sin eraser. So how do we get rid of sin's stain? Only Jesus can remove the debt we owe God. He is the doorway to heaven.

The purpose of the Old Testament laws and the Gospel is to show us how far from God's holiness we are. When we see the hardness of our hearts, we are driven to put our faith in Jesus–His precious sacrifice removing our imperfection, His righteousness standing in the place of our wrongdoing. When you admit to God that you need cleansing and want Jesus to be your Savior, not only will your soul live in heaven with Him when you die. You will also have the great joy of being set free from your need to compare yourself to other people, because of your position as His child.

CHAPTER 14
The Great Exchange
Redemption changes everything.

"Men of Israel, hear these words: Jesus of Nazareth, a man attested to you by God with mighty works and wonders and signs that God did through him in your midst, as you yourselves know— this Jesus, delivered up according to the definite plan and foreknowledge of God, you crucified and killed by the hands of lawless men. God raised him up, loosing the pangs of death, because it was not possible for him to be held by it....

"This Jesus God raised up, and of that we all are witnesses. Being therefore exalted at the right hand of God, and having received from the Father the promise of the Holy Spirit, he has poured out this that you yourselves are seeing and hearing....

"Let all the house of Israel therefore know for certain that God has made him both Lord and Christ, this Jesus whom you crucified."

Now when they heard this they were cut to the heart, and said to Peter and the rest of the apostles, "Brothers, what shall we do?" And Peter said to them, "Repent and be baptized every one of you in the name of Jesus Christ for the forgiveness of your sins, and you will receive the gift of the Holy Spirit. For the promise is for you and for your children and for all who are far off, everyone whom the Lord our God calls to himself...."

So those who received his word were baptized, and there were added that day about three thousand souls.

Acts 2:22-24, 32-33, 36-39, 41

One of my favorite pieces of furniture in my house is a repurposed cabinet. I keep my nice silverware and pretty pitchers in it as if it were fancy, but it's just a hand-me-down. The summer my husband and I got married, my resourceful mother-in-law sent us to pick up a used dresser a neighbor was selling. It was falling apart but a cute size and shape, so we brought it home. My new husband secured the wobbly frame, clear-coated the vintage pine top, and painted the cabinet a creamy white. If you saw it, you might wonder why I keep it, but that little cottage-y piece has always made me smile. Maybe because it was the first thing my husband and I worked together to redeem.

Redemption means many things—the repayment of a debt, the buying back of something, the trading of something of no value (like a paper coupon) for something of high value (like free lemonade). But it's more than repairing something or trading up. Redemption has a relational connection— someone has chosen to treasure the redeemed item. Because the object is treasured, it becomes valuable. Redemption in its purest definition is the deliverance of something from bondage or brokenness because a rescuer pays the price to buy it, simply because he or she wants it. In the case of my silverware cabinet, we paid a literal cost: a small amount to buy it from its previous owner and the price of labor, hardware, and paint to restore it to working condition. We also paid a relational cost: we chose to love and use it though it was worthless in the world's eyes.

On a spiritual level, God's redemption means that He treasures people. Jesus paid the required repayment for our sin debt—He took the wrath our sins deserved—because He wanted us to be His very own. Sadly, sometimes we don't give His rescue much attention. Perhaps it's not exciting to us

101

because we don't think we're "that bad." We're not the worst sinners. But when we see Him more clearly, we see our sin for what it is, and we suddenly need Him.

When Peter preached the first public sermon after God sent the Holy Spirit to live inside believers at Pentecost, the people who heard his message felt desperate about their sin problem. They didn't overanalyze, make excuses, or wait until another day, wondering if God was really who He claimed to be. Through Peter's words, they got a clear picture of Jesus, and the only response they had was surrendering to His love and redemption. Three-thousand people's lives were transformed that day—not only for that moment, but for the rest of their lives. When people come to Jesus, lasting changes happen on the inside: 1) we recognize sin for what it is and we decide we don't want to live under its control; 2) the old ways die and we become new—have a new heart, new drives, new goals and motivations; 3) God's Spirit enters our lives and teaches us how to think and live every day; and 4) we want to tell others what God has done.

No one can be redeemed without realizing the seriousness of his or her own sin. In the Bible, the pattern is that when people come face to face with God, they must grapple with their sin—they recognize their dirtiness in the presence of His holiness. In the Old Testament, Abram, Jacob, Moses, Elijah, and Isaiah responded to God with awe, respect, and worship (sometimes called "the fear of God"). In the New Testament, Jesus miraculously freed people from physical disease but also addressed their bondage to sin. He said to many people, "Go, and sin no more."

Repentance changes everything about your focus and drives, from self to God's Kingdom. A repentant heart says,

"God, I am so sorry. I hate my sin and adore You. I choose to turn from my selfishness and ask You to keep my heart from ever walking into that again. Be the ruler of my affections. Be the center of my attention."

> "Jesus stood up and said to her, 'Woman, where are they? Has no one condemned you?' She said, 'No one, Lord.' And Jesus said, 'Neither do I condemn you; go, and from now on sin no more.'"
> John 8:10-11

At the moment we repent and believe that Jesus is the Son of God who died and rose again to set us free, He rescues us from the penalty of sin (hell), as well as the slavery to sin. Romans 7 and 8 explain that before we know Jesus, all we know and desire is sin. But when we invite Jesus to control our heart, mind, and desires, He disconnects us from sin—kind of like He has unhitched the trailer that carried the load of shame and self-destruction we were dragging around. That trailer still exists, and we can slip up and revisit it (and we do). But we are not bound to it in any way. It is not where we get our satisfaction or identity. The bondage is severed. The shame is released like a balloon in the breeze. Because the Holy Spirit has drawn us to God and now lives inside, we have a new Master. The authority figure in our lives is no longer sin and self, but God and His Word. We can learn to let Him direct our thinking and cravings. We *can* resist the draw of sin. We can choose to honor God instead of feeling obligated to follow through on our impulses.

THE Rs OF REDEMPTION

By God's grace and the work of the Holy Spirit, God calls people to Himself to be redeemed—released from bondage, bought back from slavery to sin, and rescued from the grip of the Deceiver. It is difficult to put into words what happens inside us when we realize we need Jesus. A beautiful miracle and mystery, God reaches out to us and we respond. I've listed some concepts (in alphabetical order) to help you better understand what salvation involves.

Rebirth—God makes you alive spiritually.

Receive—You accept the truth of His Word.

Recognize—You realize your sin; you admit you have failed His holy standard and need His forgiveness.

Reconciliation—Your relationship with God is put back together.

Regeneration—God changes who you are.

Repentance—You turn from your sin.

Rescue—Jesus frees you from your bondage to sin and the punishment you deserve.

Response—You choose to confess your sin and believe that Jesus is the Son of God who died, was buried, and rose again.

Restoration—God puts your mind and heart at peace regardless of past rebellion.

Revelation—God initiates a relationship with you by revealing His holiness and truth.

Righteousness—God gives **you** credit for the good *He* has done in you.

Beyond paying the price for our punishment and severing our ties to sin, God also does a beautiful healing work in our minds when we are saved. We need time to learn our identity in Christ, but we are immediately unchained from comparison, shame, and guilt. We embrace our new identity as we meditate on (read and study) His Word. We learn to "take every thought captive to obey Christ" (2 Corinthians 10:5). It's like at first we were locked in a prison, bound by chains of sin—not only our body, but also our mind. When we ask Jesus save us, the chains are broken and the prison door is open. But we have to get up and walk out of the cell. Knowing what God says in His Word helps us move step by step out of that cell and away from our old patterns (2 Timothy 2:25-26).

> "But he was pierced for our transgressions;
> he was crushed for our iniquities;
> upon him was the chastisement that brought us peace,
> and with his wounds we are healed.
> All we like sheep have gone astray;
> we have turned—every one—to his own way;
> and the Lord has laid on him the iniquity of us all."
> Isaiah 53:5-6

As our thoughts change, our actions also change. We want to do what is right. Even though it is God who graciously helps us choose to follow Him daily, He gives us credit for those good actions. It's like if we owed a debt and someone funded the monthly bill until it was paid off, then continued making payments into an investment with our name on it, and then said, "Wow! Look at all the money you've saved up." That person did all of the work but they gave us all the benefits. That's what it looks like when God covers us in the righteousness of Jesus.

Maybe you never realized what a great exchange Jesus made for your soul. You give Him your filthy rags; He gives you new garments, white as snow, free of charge, unconditionally—because of His choice to treasure you. He wants to be your Redeemer.

God's Word compels us to see who Jesus is. You have a decision to make. We cannot say Jesus is a good teacher if we don't believe He tells the truth about being the only Savior. We can't say the Bible's principles are useful, but optional. You can't say you follow God if you don't know or do what He says. The Bible doesn't leave room for sitting in the middle. So where are you with Him right now?

- Maybe you are caught up in the Rs of refusal instead of the Rs of redemption. You **resist**, **reject**, and **rebel** against the truth of the Bible. From cussing to viewing habits, you live the way you want to live—everyone is doing what you do. If you feel no problem with sin, ask who is in charge of your life.
- Maybe you are ready to have that first conversation with God, admitting your need.
- Maybe you're at the place of sincere surrender, but struggling to believe His lavish love for you.

There is so much more we could say about the work of the Trinity. I hope what we've covered here has helped you understand and delight in Him more. Wherever you are on your journey of encountering God, I pray for you to become His daughter, claim the redemption Jesus bought for you, and experience the joy of a life lived for Him. Knowing Him is how we learn to live beyond compare.

"Therefore, if anyone is in Christ,
he is a new creation.
The old has passed away;
behold, the new has come.
All this is from God, who through Christ
reconciled us to himself
and gave us the ministry of
reconciliation."
2 Corinthians 5:17-18

Part 4

REDEFINED

LAUGH at Satan's Lies

"See how very much our Father loves us, for he calls us
his children, and that is what we are!"
1 John 3:1a, NLT

Beginning Thoughts

My goal for this book is *not* to give you ten tips to feel better about yourself. If we solved the problem of our insecurity with accomplishments and good deeds, we could win a contest, get a good grade, or show kindness to someone and be good to go. We would feel great about ourselves on our own and wouldn't question our worth.

But we do question. So we must need more than worldly success and human praise to find validation. We need a secure and steady source of approval and love.

In this part, we will learn about the new identity God has made possible for those who choose to follow Jesus. We'll find where we belong: in His Kingdom. We'll hear His promises that because we are His children, we can LAUGH at the Enemy's lies (see the acrostic below). Because of His love, not our performance, we don't have to worry or wonder about our value any longer.

TAKEAWAYS FOR PART 4

- We are **Loved**.
- We are **Approved**.
- We are **Understood**.
- We are **God-led**.
- We are **Healthy enough** to do what He wants us to do.

CHAPTER 15

Loved

To care less what people think, care more
what God thinks.

They came to the other side of the sea, to the country
of the Gerasenes. And when Jesus had stepped out of
the boat, immediately there met him out of the tombs a
man with an unclean spirit. He lived among the tombs.
And no one could bind him anymore, not even with a
chain, for he had often been bound with shackles and
chains, but he wrenched the chains apart, and he broke
the shackles in pieces. No one had the strength to
subdue him. Night and day among the tombs and on
the mountains he was always crying out and cutting
himself with stones. And when he saw Jesus from afar,
he ran and fell down before him. And crying out with a
loud voice, he said, "What have you to do with me,
Jesus, Son of the Most High God? I adjure you by God,
do not torment me." For he was saying to him, "Come
out of the man, you unclean spirit!" And Jesus asked
him, "What is your name?" He replied, "My name is
Legion, for we are many." And he begged him earnestly
not to send them out of the country. Now a great herd
of pigs was feeding there on the hillside, and they
begged him, saying, "Send us to the pigs; let us enter
them." So he gave them permission. And the unclean
spirits came out and entered the pigs; and the herd,
numbering about two thousand, rushed down the steep
bank into the sea and drowned in the sea.

The herdsmen fled and told it in the city and in the
country. And people came to see what it was that had

happened. And they came to Jesus and saw the demon-possessed man...sitting there, clothed and in his right mind, and they were afraid. And those who had seen it described to them what had happened to the demon-possessed man and to the pigs. And they began to beg Jesus to depart from their region. As he was getting into the boat, the man who had been possessed with demons begged him that he might be with him. And he did not permit him but said to him, "Go home to your friends and tell them how much the Lord has done for you, and how he has had mercy on you." And he went away and began to proclaim in the Decapolis how much Jesus had done for him, and everyone marveled.

Mark 5:1-20

My oldest child had just turned 7 when my youngest was born, old enough to be a big help. Every morning while I changed the baby and got her dressed for the day, big sis would crawl into the room meowing like a cat. The baby would start giggling and looking for her. As soon as the baby could talk, she learned to say, "Here comes da kitty!" It was kind of a silly thing, but both of them knew what it meant: security, being there, adoring each other, love. We show love in lots of ways—double-tapping on Instagram, helping a friend, writing a note. But we also need to be aware that we interpret lots of things as love that really are not love at all.

What does it mean to be loved? There is so much confusion about this word. Teenage girls, hungry for love, think being loved is having attention—*any kind* of attention. Ignored wives think love means someone wanting to spend time with them. Overworked men think love means being appreciated without someone (wife, boss) complaining. Our interpretation of love often becomes whatever we lack in our relationships. If someone would offer us what we crave, we would feel loved.

> "Here is what love is. It is not that we loved God. It is that he loved us and sent his Son to give his life to pay for our sins."
> 1 John 4:10 (NIrV)

Certainly, love means being shown attention, but it is much more than that. In 1 Corinthians 13, Paul describes love with words we easily understand: patient, kind, not boastful, not jealous or self-centered. This kind of love is a gift—and not everyone who claims they love you knows how to love like this. Sometimes "love" is offered conditionally. It is used

The world and the Enemy say that for us to be loved, we have to do something. We have to be good enough first, then maybe we can have this love we need so desperately. That's like telling a starving child he can have bread only after he runs a marathon.

WHAT ABOUT SPIRITUAL WARFARE?

In His Word, God gives glimpses of the supernatural realm: Daniel 9-10; Job 1-2; 1 Chronicles 21:1-2; Zechariah 3; Matthew 4; 1 Peter 5:8; and many more. From these verses, we see that God's angels work for His glory and the protection of His people, while Satan and his demons stand against God's people and try to lead lives astray. Demons are morally perverted and strategic in their deceit, but they are limited in their abilities and the time they have to do their wicked work.

God is the ultimate authority, and He will one day put a full stop to their work. However, now people open themselves to evil influences when they, by their choice, give up their consciousness and unite themselves to activities and people that oppose God. Examples of this include getting drunk or high; participating in witchcraft, Satanic rituals, manifestation, fortune telling, and horoscopes (Deuteronomy 18:10-14); and pursuing illicit sexual activities (1 Corinthians 6:13-20). Satan is always working to destroy us, but we can resist his lies. We can repent of our sin, sever ties to demonic activity, and align our ways with God's Word.

We don't know the reason this poor man was tangled up with demons, but Jesus knew why. He didn't come to him to accuse him; He came to set him free. *The Invisible War* by Chip Ingram is a helpful resource if you'd like to learn more about God's power over evil.

Comparison is a key part of the Enemy's strategy to defeat us. It makes us feel like everyone is more deserving, like we lack the love and affection everyone else has. We conclude it's not possible for us to be loved. And that is a lie. The truth is this: you were designed and are deeply loved by the Almighty God. He has affection for you and desires connection with you. He wants you to experience wholeness and joy and has prepared ways for you to contribute to His kingdom by impacting others' lives.

The message of the Bible is that not only is it possible for us to be loved, it is impossible *not* to be. The truest definition of love is a trustworthy person committing to care lifelong for a beloved friend's best interest, no matter what it costs. God made that commitment in the form of the sacrifice of His Son. Even before His death and resurrection, He made a permanent decision to love people and call them to Himself. At the Cross, He turned His wrath away from every single person who believes in Him—so now we can run into His forgiving arms.

"But God shows his love for us in that while we were still sinners, Christ died for us."
Romans 5:8

Our perfection and performance don't earn us this love, and our failure doesn't disqualify us from it. Love is simply a gift from God.

Before we ever looked for Him, He went to the Cross. He saw the brokenness that bound us and came to our world and initiated a relationship with us that transforms our lives.

> "So we have come to know and to believe the love that God has for us."
> 1 John 4:16

Love doesn't enter our lives when we cover our own faults with pretty karma-kindness. Love can't be bought with comparison—we don't get a little more love on those days it appears the scale is tipped our way and less when it's not. Once we've experienced His love, we naturally grow in our desire to align our lives with His Word, for His glory and our benefit, but our actions don't buy His love or increase our personal worth. Sex is not love. Likes are not love. Even attention is not love in its complete form. We experience the love we are looking for when we meet Jesus. And you can do that today.

WHEN GOOD BEHAVIOR IS BAD

People try to fill the holes in their lives not only with wrong behavior—sometimes they try to be very, very "good" people. But humans will never behave well enough to be blameless. Legalism is following Biblical commands for the wrong reasons, like to earn salvation, or following strict human-made rules based on Bible verses that are misinterpreted. Legalism doesn't change the heart, only behavior. In many ways, legalism is simply a game of comparison—comparing our external religious acts to others'. God doesn't want this pretend spirituality in our lives. He wants complete wholeness and sincere faithfulness. He wants us to admit our dependence on Jesus and fill our minds with His Word. He wants us to know that approval from people or achievements cannot fill our hearts. Our hearts were shaped for Him.

CHAPTER 16
Approved
Rejection isn't always a bad thing.

And while he was at Bethany in the house of Simon the leper, as he was reclining at table, a woman came with an alabaster flask of ointment of pure nard, very costly, and she broke the flask and poured it over his head. There were some who said to themselves indignantly, "Why was the ointment wasted like that? For this ointment could have been sold for more than three hundred denarii and given to the poor." And they scolded her. But Jesus said, "Leave her alone. Why do you trouble her? She has done a beautiful thing to me. For you always have the poor with you, and whenever you want, you can do good for them. But you will not always have me. She has done what she could; she has anointed my body beforehand for burial. And truly, I say to you, wherever the gospel is proclaimed in the whole world, what she has done will be told in memory of her."

Then Judas Iscariot, who was one of the twelve, went to the chief priests in order to betray him to them.

Mark 14:3-10

I was helping in a seventh grade language arts class one day when the teacher passed out the assignment. It was a page entitled, "All About Me," and the students were supposed to fill in boxes with favorite hobbies, foods, and people, and, at the bottom of the page, a description of their personality—how their friends saw them and how they saw themselves. I was sitting with Jolie* and helped her write a few things in each box. When we got to the last one, her face became like a stone and she wouldn't answer. After a few awkward minutes, she mumbled, "Dumb, dumb, dumb." Jolie was a funny, creative student, liked by her classmates. But all she could call herself was dumb. When I started describing how I saw her interact with others—someone who always spoke encouraging words, someone who could make people laugh and smile with her stories and presence in the room—she started to cry. I said, "Can you see this about yourself? You are special to your friends." She shook her head no and mumbled, "All I ever see is dumb," and she refused to write anything in the box.

I grieve for Jolie and for every person who can't fill that box with a meaningful description, yet I have been there, too. When we don't hear approving words from the people around us, and sometimes even when we do, we wonder what people think, and sometimes we make up a tragic story about our worthlessness, because that's how we feel on the inside.

In Mark 14, adoration (gratitude, respect, and love mixed together) moved a woman named Mary (Martha and Lazarus' sister) to bring an extravagant gift to Jesus. She presented the gift in an unusual way. Instead of sitting quietly in the background, she bravely cracked open a bottle of perfume that cost almost a year's wages. She approached Jesus and

*Name changed

119

poured the luxury liquid over His head. I can picture Jesus sitting there, eyes closed, as the liquid tickled His scalp and ran down His hair. I can picture Him smiling at His dear friend and nodding, knowing what she was communicating with the gift—that He was worth more than all her possessions. She was anointing Him for what was coming next. Amidst the sacred atmosphere of this loving gesture, other people started criticizing her! Scripture says they scolded her.

Jesus' response to their criticism is precious. He said, "Leave her alone. Why are you bothering her?" (Mark 14:6, HCSB). Then He gave them the same charge of doing what they complained she should do—He told them to help the poor. Then—don't miss this—He told the dinner party that her act of sacrificial worship, the story of her gift, would be retold all over the world. Maybe she shook her head, thinking, "That's not necessary." But here we are, sharing it now.

Affirmation = encouraging words about your importance and ability to contribute, being approved by someone verbally

---

If the woman was looking for the crowd's approval when she gave her gift, she surely didn't find it. But that's not what she was after. She wasn't looking for approval at all—she was *thanking* Jesus for the peace and love she had found in Him. She was focused on worshipping and elevating Him, not herself. Interestingly, in laying down her search for human approval, she received lasting approval from a lasting God.

Jesus called the human critics' complaining what it was: a bother. Their loud opinions didn't change His mind. In this case, rejection wasn't negative: the sincere woman was rejected by humans who misunderstood her act of worship, but she was accepted by Jesus, who completely received her gift. Rejection often isn't a bad thing, though we fear it a lot. We make the mistake of thinking rejection means we are wrong or insignificant. Actually, rejection from certain groups may confirm we are doing the right thing and that our actions are having great impact. It's tempting to waste our whole lives working for the approval of people who 1) don't know us, 2) aren't worthy of that much power over our lives, and 3) keep changing the rules. Isn't it better to do what God affirms and stop worrying about being rejected by people?

Notice it is this interaction that immediately precedes Judas going to make arrangements with the chief priests to betray Jesus. Why did the woman's gift trigger such deep resentment in him? Clearly, he couldn't accept correction or conviction. But it was more than that—Judas couldn't stand Jesus' generous approval of human beings who were "not worthy." He was so consumed with greed and pride that it literally skewed the way he thought of other humans. In the end, although he traveled with Jesus, he did not agree with Him on the worth Jesus gave to each individual.

THEY DIDN'T TELL ME I WAS SPECIAL

No matter how it feels, a person's failure to show you unconditional love or affirmation does not mean you are not worthy of love and approval. Their inability to affirm you may stem from their background or selfish choices, or simply unintentional insensitivity. We cannot depend on human approval for feeling good about ourselves. It's time to change the narrative in our head and hearts. God has already decided your immeasurable worth. It's time to listen to Him instead of looking to others for the affirmation our hearts need.

Approval is the first thing people withdraw in relationships when they are mad or jealous. We raise our eyebrows, roll our eyes, crinkle our nose, turn our back, and whisper to the next person. We actually physically reject people. We know how to emotionally disapprove of people, too. Distance. Not responding. Talking with everyone except the person who wants our friendship.

I think approval is the first thing to go in relationships because we sort of instinctively know that if we withhold it, it will hurt and send people in a tailspin—and that's what we want it to do. Our Enemy knows it hurts, too. One disapproving look can unsettle our whole week. So Satan tempts us, in big and little ways, to intentionally withhold affirmation from one another—from outright critiques to simple distractions, where we casually neglect (not meaning to be rude, just never getting around to) really life-changing things like encouraging one another.

Most of the time, our sense of not being approved comes from real relationships that have been fractured. It can, however, come from a *perceived* place. This happens when we allow lies to reside in our minds and we don't stop them—the people around us do affirm us but we refuse to receive it.

And maybe it is our fear of rejection that makes us resist hearing from God about areas He wants to change in our lives. It feels like He's dismissing us when something we want to do is not approved by Him. But that's not what happens in conviction. God actually works to draw people to Himself, not push them away. There's a huge difference in God's disapproval of sin and His approval of you as a person. God hates sin because it leads to brokenness. God's concern for your holiness leads to your wholeness and closeness to Him. That's what He wants for you.

Regardless of inferiority's source, the sense of not being approved of is one of the most powerful forces in all of history—we've seen how it leads people astray. The good news is, God gives approval in ways humans can't. And He has a precious purpose for approval. First Thessalonians 2:4 says, "We have been approved by God to be entrusted with the gospel, so we speak, not to please man, but to please God who tests our hearts." Ultimately, the reason and source for approval are the same: knowing Jesus and introducing others to Him. May the Lord help us live that out.

SOCIAL MEDIA AND THE REJECTION EPIDEMIC

Friend rejection issues are causing more problems now than ever. Social media like Instagram and Snapchat announce where and when groups of friends get together. Those who are left out know they weren't invited. Sometimes people leave comments that wreck bonds. Friendships and hearts are broken.

I have gotten my feelings hurt online; I'm sure you have too. I'm also sure that sometimes those who hurt my feelings online did not mean to and had no idea they were doing so. Nor have I ever meant to hurt others with posts, but my guess is I have. That's the nature of posts—they are quick, relatively thoughtless, and for fun. But they can hurt so much.

Sometimes I have to take a step back from social media and remind myself to use it as the tool for good that it can be, not as a smoothie blender for my esteem. For thousands of years, the world lived without knowing everyone's thoughts and location. Perhaps, today may be one day you don't need to read what's going on— especially if it threatens to undo what God's Word did in your heart this morning.

CHAPTER 17

Understood

What God knows is more important than what people assume.

And in his teaching he said, "Beware of the scribes, who like to walk around in long robes and like greetings in the marketplaces and have the best seats in the synagogues and the places of honor at feasts, who devour widows' houses and for a pretense make long prayers. They will receive the greater condemnation."

And he sat down opposite the treasury and watched the people putting money into the offering box. Many rich people put in large sums. And a poor widow came and put in two small copper coins, which make a penny. And he called his disciples to him and said to them, "Truly, I say to you, this poor widow has put in more than all those who are contributing to the offering box. For they all contributed out of their abundance, but she out of her poverty has put in everything she had, all she had to live on."

Mark 12:38-44

I told you a little about my husband's grandfather. He's the one who repaired the church ceiling. Thomas White lived to be 101. As a young man he farmed, worked in land moving, and sold insurance. Then, he was an auctioneer for more than 60 years, helping people buy and sell property and goods that enriched their lives. How did he end up in the adventurous career he loved so much? One weekend, Thomas attended an auction and the auctioneer didn't show up. A community doctor, someone who had given Thomas opportunities before, saw him in the crowd and asked him to cry the auction. The doc told Thomas it would help the family. "I can't do something like that," Thomas tried to argue. His mentor replied, "Thomas, you can do anything." Having someone he admired so much tell him he *could* gave him the courage to stand up and start the auction. And he didn't stop until near the end of his long life.

One of the greatest feelings in life is when someone gets us—understands our heart and sees abilities and strengths in us that we don't even realize we have. One of the worst feelings is when someone doesn't get us—like they're confused by what we're trying to say or seem weirded out by our personality. I remember many times sitting in a job training, a new class, or church meeting where I felt awkward and different from everyone else there, like they thought I was odd. Have you ever felt that way?

Picture the courage of the widow in Mark 12. When she came to the temple to worship, she knew she didn't have much to bring. She may have even been ridiculed or scolded by the priests at times because she had so little to give. Still, the widow went to worship. Still, she gave, because pleasing God was more important to her than pleasing people. And Jesus took notice and praised her beautiful heart publicly.

My guess is, Jesus' warning about the scribes wasn't random. I wonder if He knew she had personally experienced the phrase "devour widow's houses." Throughout history and in the culture of the Jesus' day, people with power used deceptive tactics to take advantage of others. For example, they might make a loan with astronomical interest. Or claim something was owed that wasn't, then take a widow's house as payment for the debt they'd made up. They might let the widow continue living in the house they took, but they would charge rent. I wonder if someone in the temple at the very moment Jesus was there had committed fraud against this innocent, faithful woman. It might have even been someone making a lengthy prayer or giving a big offering. Those who perform like they're perfect aren't always genuine in how they treat people. Jesus understood the boasting and manipulation of the powerful and the humble purity of the widow.

Shallow and showy or authentic and unseen, we cannot hide our motivations from God. I think the widow knew this—*really* knew and trusted God to be her defender against those who mistreated her. Her gift was way more than two half-pennies. It was her statement of faith that she believed God saw her and would provide for her. She gave Him *all* of her security and provision, and He gave her all of His attention. The widow could have latched onto the accusations, mistreatment, and unkindness of people in her community. She could have lived believing their lies. She could have spent her years focused on winning their approval or trying to get back what they stole. Instead, she made a resolute decision to trust God without bitterness toward her oppressors, without withdrawing from community, and without apology for who she was.

It's not easy to get to the place this amazing lady did—surrendering our right to defend ourselves and giving our reputation to God. If I could have a cup of coffee with the widow, I'd ask how she became so confident in the Lord. But I think we already have her answer. Perhaps she'd pat my hand and say with a smile, "You can give your worries to God. He is bigger than those people who are too big for their britches, and He is certainly big enough to take care of you."

The widow surrendered her right to be angry at her oppressors. She also refused to agree with them. They treated her as unworthy, like she wasn't able to impress God the way *they* were. But the way she continued to worship indicates their contempt failed to change her mind about herself or God. She had great joy and trust in God despite the circumstances of life. I often fall into thinking untrue and unkind things about myself at the suggestion of oppressors. I want to live more like the widow, focused on the Father instead of looking around to see who is watching.

The priests and scribes said some important-sounding, long prayers, but Jesus pointed out that their assessment of themselves (and others) was a bit twisted. People in our community, family, and circle of friends talk, too. I've never met anyone who wasn't eager to share his or her opinion. People always have something to say. So don't let your emotions get caught up in the opinions of others without ever considering whether they are well-informed.

A few years ago, I was struggling with feeling looked down on by a close friend. I felt like anything I did was not good enough. I don't know if it was her judgy attitude or my insecurity, but I was really bothered that I couldn't please her. The Lord showed me a verse in the Bible that changed my outlook: "For now we see in a mirror dimly, but then face to face. Now I know in part; then I shall know fully, even as I have been fully known" (1 Corinthians 13:12). Though this friend knew me, her vision of my life was kind of like a foggy mirror. Jesus' understanding of me is crystal clear and complete. He designed my personality, pace, and set of talents. He shaped my interests, passion, and compassion. He sees when I cry—He even collects all my tears! He knows me fully, beautifully. So when I face the criticism, ridicule, and rejection of humans, I can have confidence and know He has a purpose for me. (This verse also reminds me I don't always see others as plainly as God does. I need to be careful not to be judgy, because He created and loves each person.)

"You...put my tears in your bottle.
Are they not in Your book?"
Psalm 56:8

Just like the widow in the temple, we face the chatter of people every day. How can we follow her example and push back words that want to worm their way into our hearts and eat us from the inside out?

Scripture urges us to weigh the accusations we hear. Filter others' words prayerfully. Consider whether they are true, right, kind, and useful (2 Corinthians 10:5, Philippians 4:8). Remember that people often talk before they think—they say misinformed and untrue things.

God's goal for our lives is not to please everyone around us. It is to please Him. His love gives us the courage to listen to His Words above everyone else's.

A WORD ABOUT RECEIVING CORRECTION

We will not do everything right in our growing walk with God. He knows I've made some ridiculously self-centered decisions. I've made stupid comments. Sometimes what I need is a good word of correction. When correction comes from a wise friend who has put effort into understanding you, don't become defensive or cut them off. Listen. If someone cares and wants you to have a blessed future, that is a gift.

The reason correction has hurt so much in the past is that we thought we had to be perfect to be loved, and criticism meant someone thought we weren't. Now that we know perfection is not the goal, we don't have to fear the constructive comments of others. Another reason correction hurt was because we were believing *everyone's* opinions—even those of people who were misinformed. Now we know to look to Jesus for the assurance of our value. We don't have to base our value on human opinions, which change with every person and day.

CHAPTER 18

God-Led

When we see God is worth more than anything else, we step in the right direction.

King Nebuchadnezzar made an image of gold, whose height was sixty cubits and its breadth six cubits. He set it up on the plain of Dura, in the province of Babylon. Then King Nebuchadnezzar sent to gather the satraps, the prefects, and the governors, the counselors, the treasurers, the justices, the magistrates, and all the officials of the provinces to come to the dedication of the image that King Nebuchadnezzar had set up.... And they stood before the image that Nebuchadnezzar had set up. And the herald proclaimed aloud, "You are commanded, O peoples, nations, and languages, that when you hear the sound of the horn, pipe, lyre, trigon, harp, bagpipe, and every kind of music, you are to fall down and worship the golden image that King Nebuchadnezzar has set up. And whoever does not fall down and worship shall immediately be cast into a burning fiery furnace." Therefore, as soon as all the peoples heard the sound of the horn, pipe, lyre, trigon, harp, bagpipe, and every kind of music, all the peoples, nations, and languages fell down and worshiped the golden image that King Nebuchadnezzar had set up. Therefore at that time certain Chaldeans came forward and maliciously accused the Jews. They declared to King Nebuchadnezzar, "O king, live forever! You, O king, have made a decree, that every man who hears the sound of the horn, pipe, lyre, trigon, harp, bagpipe, and every kind of music, shall fall down and worship the golden image. And whoever does not fall down and worship shall be cast into a burning fiery furnace. There are certain Jews whom you have appointed over the affairs of the province of Babylon: Shadrach, Meshach, and Abednego. These men, O king, pay no attention to you; they do not serve your gods or worship the golden image that you have set up."

Then Nebuchadnezzar in furious rage commanded that Shadrach, Meshach, and Abednego be brought. So they brought these men before the king. Nebuchadnezzar answered and said to them, "Is it true, O Shadrach, Meshach, and Abednego, that you do not serve my gods or worship the golden image that I have set up? Now if you are ready when you hear the sound of the horn, pipe, lyre, trigon, harp, bagpipe, and every kind of music, to fall down and worship the image that I have made, well and good. But if you do not worship, you shall immediately be cast into a burning fiery furnace. And who is the god who will deliver you out of my hands?"

Shadrach, Meshach, and Abednego answered and said to the king, "O Nebuchadnezzar, we have no need to answer you in this matter. If this be so, our God whom we serve is able to deliver us from the burning fiery furnace, and he will deliver us out of your hand, O king. But if not, be it known to you, O king, that we will not serve your gods or worship the golden image that you have set up."

Daniel 3:1-17

I've had pet cats all my life, but I have never loved one as much as the cat I have now. His name is Puppy, and I send a picture of him to my adult children almost every day. He sleeps beside me as I write and follows me into the kitchen when I get snacks. He's almost always with me, but sometimes he likes to go outside and chase baby chipmunks in the yard. If he doesn't come when I call, I shake a bag of Temptations® cat treats. You've never seen a cat turn into a bullet like Puppy when the treat bag rattles. Although Puppy loves me (as much as a cat can love), I must sadly admit, he is led by his appetite. He'd follow anyone who has the treat bag.

Who or what leads your life?

Are you money-led, getting a degree where the biggest salary is, spending your energy—your life—on a career for the financial reward rather than genuine passion for it?

Are you friend-led, doing what people tell you to do?

Are you parent-led or extended family-led, a young adult still trying to secure approval that your loved ones don't unconditionally offer?

Are you insecurity-led, doing whatever your anxious thoughts tell you to do today to fit in and please others?

Are you led by social media, living for likes and comments and a pretty Insta feed?

Are you pride-led, trying to do great things—even "for God"—so you can be at the top?

If you're a mom, are you kid-led, doing whatever your kids beg you to do right when they whine for you to do it?

Are you, like Puppy, led by your cravings, looking for substances or thrills to fill up the holes in your heart?

Ouch, that's enough. All of us can point to specific decisions in our lives when we were led by something other than God. Today, many of us deal with lingering consequences of those times we didn't let Him be in charge. So what does it mean to be God-led? Let's look at the example of Shadrach, Meshach, and Abednego.

Shadrach, Meshach, and Abednego were not strangers to King Nebuchadnezzar, the king of Babylon. The king had kidnapped them and dozens of other good-looking, educated people from Jerusalem when his army defeated the Jewish people. (God had warned this would happen because of their rebellion against Him, and it did.)

Not everyone who was captured had strayed from God. God had a plan to use the boldness of a few to impact a nation that would otherwise never have heard and seen such amazing things about God: the people of Babylon (now Iraq) saw these three young men and Daniel, Esther, Mordecai, and Nehemiah delivered in dramatic ways. God allowed them to rise to positions of leadership and influence, and each of them used their platform to fearlessly prove that God was the one true God in the middle of a pagan nation.

King Nebuchadnezzar had encountered Shadrach, Meshach, Abednego, and their friend Daniel when they were first captured. The king wanted the captives to be educated and well fed from his big buffet for three years. The problem was, the buffet had a lot of food that God had instructed His people to avoid. So Daniel and his friends asked for permission *not* to eat from the buffet. From the very start, they did not apologize for believing God's authority and law. They didn't back down from their faith, and they didn't give in to Babylon's culture.

So when Nebuchadnezzar pridefully built his giant golden sculpture of himself, they had already decided they weren't going to worship anyone but God. Their character was set.

When tattle-tales told the king they weren't bowing down, they were ready to face the king's furnace. Regardless of how God worked—whether He delivered them or not—they remained God-led.

> "Trust in the Lord with all your heart, and do not lean on your own understanding. In all your ways acknowledge him, and he will make straight your paths."
> Proverbs 3:5-6

The stories of the lives of these brave young men show something about their relationship with God that I think we are missing today. Today, we're told to do whatever is necessary to keep our image intact, that our self-worth is higher priority than anything else. But these men recognized something crucial about living without intimidation: **they were in existence to serve God; He wasn't there to serve them.** They loved God, and they revered Him—set Him and His words and ways higher than anything else, including their own sense of esteem. Interestingly, they became such important leaders in Babylon that others were jealous and tried extreme tactics to take them down. They didn't change who or what led their lives to get or keep their positions. They didn't cling to them, either. They saw God had purpose in their jobs, so they did them well, but they were literally ready to die if they had to choose between following God or people.

Open your Bible and read the rest of Daniel 3. God shows up in the fire with the three young men, and when they walk out of the flames, they don't even smell like smoke. They are promoted at work (again). And Nebuchadnezzar made a new law that no one can speak badly about God. In a land where there were many gods, the king declared that no god was like the one true God. Wow. I want to live with that kind of conviction. If we don't, what will others see of God?

Being God-led doesn't mean we are perfect. There is no way to be faultless in our discernment, actions, and knowledge. We cannot know or do it all. But we can be intentional in living for Him. Being God-led means we prioritize Him in all our decisions—we get our direction from Him and from our desire to honor Him. It means we are fearless and bold, and that we care more about pleasing Him than pleasing people, even people in power.

Being God-led means that though we may not always start with the right response, we'll move to His way of thinking. Being God-led means we let Him speak to us through His Word instead of resisting instruction.

Being God-led means, again and again, our character is marked by Christ, and people notice. It means we relocate our source of identity. Being God-led means we want to glorify God more than anything else, because we've come to see that He is worth more than anything else.

Romans 8:14-17 explains that when we let God lead, His Spirit breaks our constant slavery to inferiority, insecurity, and intimidation. Knowing that we belong to God, that we are His child and even a fellow heir with Christ, sets us free. **Heir** is a little word with huge significance. It means we are legally God's children. It means Christ shares with us everything He has inherited from God the Father—not only in heaven one day, but also now, we have everything we need to do the holy and helpful things He wants us to do.

Some people want to take all the good without the responsibilities, though. They like hearing all the great things God says about them without caring a thing about God's Word or repentance. I fear some people have gotten the wrong message about being a child of the King. Belonging to God's family is not automatic. Though He created and loves every human being, we do not become His child until we decide to turn from sin and believe that Jesus is the Son of God. We can't claim to identify with Him if we don't agree to put Him before everything else in our lives. Being a daughter of God means we let Him lead, even if it leads to a furnace, because we trust His authority and love.

"For all who are led by the Spirit of God are sons of God. For you did not receive the spirit of slavery to fall back into fear, but you have received the Spirit of adoption as sons, by whom we cry, 'Abba! Father!' The Spirit himself bears witness with our spirit that we are children of God, and if children, then heirs—heirs of God and fellow heirs with Christ."
Romans 8:14-17

If we are led by the treat bag, we'll end up with a little surface satisfaction, and probably a *lot* of brokenness. If we are led by comparison, we'll end up where people, not God, want us to go. When we're God-led, we'll end up in the right place, even when people tell us we're going the wrong way. We must start getting our direction from *God*, not friends. We worship One. We live for One. We answer to One. We must guard our hearts from being led by anything other than God.

CHAPTER 19
Healthy Enough to Do What He Asks
Our limitations don't limit God.

As he passed by, he saw a man blind from birth. And his disciples asked him, "Rabbi, who sinned, this man or his parents, that he was born blind?" Jesus answered, "It was not that this man sinned, or his parents, but that the works of God might be displayed in him." ...Having said these things, he spit on the ground and made mud with the saliva. Then he anointed the man's eyes with the mud and said to him, "Go, wash in the pool of Siloam" (which means Sent). So he went and washed and came back seeing.

The neighbors and those who had seen him before as a beggar were saying, "Is this not the man who used to sit and beg?" Some said, "It is he." Others said, "No, but he is like him." He kept saying, "I am the man." So they said to him, "Then how were your eyes opened?" He answered, "The man called Jesus made mud and anointed my eyes and said to me, 'Go to Siloam and wash.' So I went and washed and received my sight...."

They brought to the Pharisees the man who had formerly been blind.... Some of the Pharisees said, "This man is not from God, for he does not keep the Sabbath." But others said, "How can a man who is a sinner do such signs?" And there was a division among them....

The Jews did not believe that he had been blind and had received his sight, until they called the parents of the man who had received his sight and asked them, "Is this your son, who you say was born blind? How then does he now see?" His parents answered, "We know that this is our son and that he was born blind. But how he now sees we do not know, nor do we know who opened his eyes. Ask him; he is of age. He will speak for himself." (His parents said these things because they feared the Jews)....

So for the second time they called the man who had been blind and said to him, "Give glory to God. We know that this man is a sinner." He answered, "Whether he is a sinner I do not know. One thing I do know, that though I was blind, now I see." They said to him, "What did he do to you? How did he open your eyes?" He answered them, "I have told you already, and you would not listen. Why do you want to hear it again? Do you also want to become his disciples?" And they reviled him, saying, "You are his disciple, but we are disciples of Moses. We know that God has spoken to Moses, but as for this man, we do not know where he comes from." The man answered, "Why, this is an amazing thing! You do not know where he comes from, and yet he opened my eyes. We know that God does not listen to sinners, but if anyone is a worshiper of God and does his will, God listens to him. Never since the world began has it been heard that anyone opened the eyes of a man born blind. If this man were not from God, he could do nothing." They answered him, "You were born in utter sin, and would you teach us?" And they cast him out.

Jesus heard that they had cast him out, and having found him he said, "Do you believe in the Son of Man?" He answered, "And who is he, sir, that I may believe in him?" Jesus said to him, "You have seen him, and it is he who is speaking to you." He said, "Lord, I believe," and he worshiped him.

John 9:1-38

I wish I could introduce you to my friend Kristy B. You'd love her sense of humor, way with words, and ability to understand you right away. She runs "A Novel Bee," a Facebook community of 8K followers that encourages authors and promotes new books. She is a published author herself, has won awards for poetry, and is friends with some cool Christian music artists. If that's all you knew, you'd be excited to meet her. But there's one more thing you should know—Kristy has cerebral palsy (CP) and has been nearly bedridden for about 10 years. How, you may ask, does she know so many people?! Kristy B. hasn't let her limitations limit her attitude, personal development, and pursuit of the things she loves, even though she wrestles with debilitating pain every day. Her disabilities have prepared her for the ministry God has for her. She is healthy enough to bring glory to God with her life, and so are you.

My precious relative Josie goes to dialysis three times a week to stay healthy but she's always busy preparing meals for sick people in her church and community. "I want them to know they're not alone and that someone is thinking of them," she says. Her huge heart is impressive, but there's one more thing you should know about Josie—she lost one leg to diabetes about 15 years ago. She does all her cooking and organizing from a wheelchair. Josie hasn't stopped living and making a difference for Jesus.

Even though we are often ashamed of our limitations, if we will relax and let God speak to us, we will find that setbacks and sicknesses are among the most valuable things God uses to teach us more about Him and impact others. They can shape *us* in good ways—they can give us wisdom and compassion. They can shape *others*—people see that God helps us in our down times, and they want His

139

companionship, too. *OR*…disease and disappointments can make us timid and bitter if we don't guard against it.

In John 9, we meet a man whose lifelong blindness could have made him very bitter. Not only did he struggle with a disability, but the community also gossiped about him—they said the blindness was caused by sin. They gave him as many labels as a reused Amazon box.

Instead of making the man timid, though, it seems his blindness made him fearless. It helped him see people more accurately than people with sight. He wasn't afraid when Jesus put mud on his eyes. He wasn't afraid to believe that when he washed the mud away, his eyes would be restored. Then, when he could finally see, people he'd heard and smelled all his life in the temple courtyard—gossips and priests and church leaders who'd given him coins and said their long prayers for everyone to hear—he wasn't intimidated by them. They called him and questioned him, thinking their panel could bully him into saying Jesus was a sinner and he was, too. But he wasn't so easily manipulated. They tried to get his parents on board, but they were so afraid of the people in power that they let their son handle it. So they called the healed man a second time. And this time he pushed back more: "Why do you want me to tell you the story of my healing again? You must love the stories of Jesus. Do you want to become his followers?"

Even when he was blind, I think he could see the character of this group. When they wanted to use him and abuse him, he saw it and stood up for himself and his Healer. When Jesus revealed to the healed man that He was the promised Messiah, he recognized it to be true. His disability had prepared him for faith and ministry that he may have never experienced had he always seen perfectly well.

By the way, did you notice in this story that no one agreed about who Jesus or the healed man was? So many views floated around the chatter mill. This is further proof that we shouldn't put too much stock in human opinion—who has the right to decide what another person is worth?

Limitations (disease, disability, weakness, financial need) **do not mean** God's love for us is limited. Often, that's when amazing works of God are displayed. Limitations do not mean that our ability to impact others is limited. People who work for God even when they are weak perhaps have a clearer sense of urgency than people who are healthy, rich, educated, attractive, and face minimal trials. When all is well, we tend to take our blessings for granted and keep wanting more, instead of using our resources to make any kind of impact at all.

So how can we think about limitations? We should not beg for them to happen—they will come naturally. But we should not be as afraid of them as we have been. Paul explained weakness this way: "A thorn was given me in the flesh, a messenger of Satan to harass me, to keep me from becoming conceited. Three times I pleaded with the Lord about this, that it should leave me. But he said to me, 'My grace is sufficient for you, for my power is made perfect in weakness.' Therefore I will boast all the more gladly of my weaknesses, so that the power of Christ may rest upon me. For the sake of Christ, then, I am content with weaknesses, insults, hardships, persecutions, and calamities. For when I am weak, then I am strong" (2 Corinthians 12:7b-10).

God could have taken away Paul's problem. Paul had faith, and he was persistent in prayer. God had the power. But He allowed the weakness to remain. One reason, Paul said, was to keep him humble. Another reason: so God and

141

His power would be seen instead of Paul. I'm not saying every time God allows a difficulty, it is to humble us. Paul said God specifically told him that was the reason for this trial. Ours may come for other reasons or from other sources.

HOW DO WE PRAY IN TIMES OF TRIAL?

The Bible never says, "Forget about praying. It doesn't do any good." Jesus encourages us and gives the example of boldly asking for what we need in prayer. Prayer should be our number one response to trials, but we get mixed up when we equate comfort and prosperity with His love. We often assume that what we ask for in prayer is the best possible thing. We ask for health when we are sick, financial blessings, favor with people, good grades, good times, and a good reputation. It is okay to ask God for these things. But if I'm honest, often I ask for these things because they are easy, not because I'm convinced they will bring God the most glory. If we get an attitude in prayer (in other words, get mad when God doesn't answer prayer our way), then we're putting faith in our own agenda, not in God. The goal is to move from our tight grip of control on things and trust His ability to work beyond all we can ask or think (Ephesians 3:20). So here's an attitude checklist for asking God to help in weakness:
1. Believe that nothing is impossible for God.
2. Believe that God is listening.
3. Check your motivations and attitude.
4. Make glorifying God a greater goal than personal comfort or popularity.
5. Trust that if God doesn't answer what you ask, He will use today—perhaps more than if you got what you asked.

Sometimes difficulties are the result of the sin of another person; such mistreatment breaks the heart of God. Sometimes a trial is part of living in a fallen world—stuffy noses, canceled events, and flat tires happen. Whatever the reason or source, the common purpose in limitations is for God to be put on display as the more glorious One.

For so long, our culture has equated power and perfection with physical and financial greatness. We think God wants to use only "good, successful" people. When we rely on these things, we trick ourselves with the illusion that we humans can actually have or be enough. But we can't be enough in ourselves; we need God's help. God doesn't follow worldly standards. He doesn't say only perfectly healthy, relationally unscathed, and rich people can participate in His Kingdom. Revelation 22:17b (HCSB) says, "Whoever desires should take the living water as a gift." All are welcome to choose Him as Savior and Lord.

When God doesn't answer prayers to relieve our weakness, we sometimes think He's made a mistake or He doesn't care or He can't use us now. But perhaps it is our very weakness He uses to reveal His grace to the watching world— perhaps His delay is for His glory. If God doesn't answer our prayers to deliver us, we have to believe He is great enough to use our trials to make a greater difference than healing or prosperity would. God is all-knowing and all-loving. If He allows weakness, loss, or deep disappointment, we can be assured He will bring something better out of the trial than if the trial had not happened. He will be glorified. That's a new perspective for us, but God can be trusted.

The blind man could have been born with sight. Lazarus didn't have to die when he got sick in John 11. The bleeding woman in Matthew 9 could have been healed by a doctor. But if none of these people ever struggled, would they ever have met Jesus?

You may think life would be better without the pain you've faced. Without being insensitive to the heavy burdens you may carry, may I ask, how do you know for sure that your life would be better off? The pain you've had may actually have prevented more pain. You may have become passionate or compassionate about an issue or people group because of your past, and God can use that to transform lives for eternity. God may give you wisdom because of your pain. God may allow you to know Him more intimately, take you to places in your heart and His Word that you would never have travelled without that crisis.

I tend to think winning is better than losing. Succeeding is better than failing. We've all been conditioned to think this way. The world tells us that to receive love, we have to earn it. To be approved, we have to be amazing. But what do we really gain when we achieve perfection, win, and earn medals—I mean, really? I love to win—we all do. But besides bragging rights or a plaque or ribbon, we do not grow by winning. We gain as much or more by trying, losing, and having to try again. And people remember who we are more than what we've won. That we invited others to join in team success more than that we did what we did by ourselves. Maybe we've got it all wrong believing that we must have it all together to make a difference in others' lives.

There are limits to what we can do, and we may even have big failures, but life was never about our ability anyway. God is not limited by our limitations, so let's ask Him to be at work. You are healthy enough to do all He calls you to do.

DOES GOD SEE MY PAIN?

The mistreatment of other humans is wrong. God does not cause it, He teaches against it, and He does not approve of it. Even when God redeems (restores) a life damaged by an evil person and uses this changed life in big ways, still, the pain should never have happened. When we use our pain as an excuse to walk away from God, we put ourselves in control and usually make decisions that inflict more pain in our lives and in the lives of others. Past pain does not have to destroy our ability to live for Him.

The Bible promises one day, evil will be put out of God's presence forever. Those who have suffered injustice will be vindicated (Matthew 5:11-12). Those who have lost will experience utter fulfillment. All scores will be settled. All debts will be paid. All anger will be erased. All sickness healed. All darkness, gone (Revelation 21:4, 23). I don't know how He's going to figure all that out, but His wisdom is limitless, and I trust His promises.

Until that day, we live here and now. The good news is, our purpose is not to have picture-perfect lives. Our purpose is to point people to God and say how great He is. We can do that when we are sick and when we wrestle with the question, "Why did you allow this, God?" We can do that when friends betray us or we have no money or energy to give. Our weaknesses do not disqualify us; they are like a magnifying glass showing the world Jesus.

If you have been impacted by others' evil choices, I am so sorry you were mistreated. I want you to know that you don't have to compare yourself to anyone as you travel this journey of knowing God more. Jesus Christ has more authority than those who hurt you, and He has decided that you are loved, approved, understood, God-led, and healthy enough to be a vibrant part of His kingdom.

Part 5

WATCH FOR IVY

Know What You're Choosing

"For freedom, Christ set us free. Stand firm then and
don't submit again to a yoke of slavery."
Galatians 5:1

Beginning Thoughts

On the surface, ivy is green and pretty. It creeps and climbs, seeming to decorate buildings and gardens with its lush cover. Underneath its waxy leaves, though, small tendrils give it the ability to aggressively take over, steal nourishment from hosts, and crumble walls. In a word, ivy sucks life out of what it feeds on. Ivy cares more about itself than its host. Domination is the end game.

In this part, we look under the surface of people, pursuits, and thought patterns that have acted like ivy in our lives—things that look good on the surface but are draining us of vitality and confidence. Sometimes the ivy has crept up on us outside of our control—like when a person tries to take advantage of your kindness. Sometimes the ivy is something we cultivate by our own choices and attitudes—like when we resist giving up the habit that's draining our joy. Either way, ivy keeps us dragged down with an incorrect view of God's abilities and our own.

Maybe no one ever told you—you are allowed to stop ivy. As you learn more about God's Word and His heart, your wisdom and confidence will grow. I hope this part helps you see and uproot the ivy in your life.

TAKEAWAYS FOR PART 5

- People, pursuits, and thought patterns can act like ivy.
- With the power of the Holy Spirit, we can cut off the control we give to ivy people in our minds and hearts.
- With God's help, we can learn to stop destructive thought patterns.

CHAPTER 20
Ivy That Entangles
Giving in doesn't detangle ivy.

Now Sarai, Abram's wife, had borne him no children. She had a female Egyptian servant whose name was Hagar. And Sarai said to Abram, "Behold now, the Lord has prevented me from bearing children. Go in to my servant; it may be that I shall obtain children by her." And Abram listened to the voice of Sarai. So, after Abram had lived ten years in the land of Canaan, Sarai, Abram's wife, took Hagar the Egyptian, her servant, and gave her to Abram her husband as a wife. And he went in to Hagar, and she conceived. And when she saw that she had conceived, she looked with contempt on her mistress. And Sarai said to Abram, "May the wrong done to me be on you! I gave my servant to your embrace, and when she saw that she had conceived, she looked on me with contempt. May the Lord judge between you and me!" But Abram said to Sarai, "Behold, your servant is in your power; do to her as you please." Then Sarai dealt harshly with her, and she fled from her.

Genesis 16:1-6

"I don't know why you didn't wear what I told you to wear. This is a bridal shower, not a baby shower, and you look six months pregnant." I couldn't believe my ears when I overheard a young friend's mother spitting out these attacking words as they walked into the shower being hosted in her honor. Her mom calmed down and put on a plastic-y sweetness for the party, but I noticed several times she made jabs at the decisions, appearance, and abilities of her beautiful, smart adult daughter—not in response to anything wrong the daughter did or said, just out of the blue. In between jabs, she would say something sappy and endearing to pull her daughter's heart close to her again, to gain her trust, then she'd break her heart again with another critique. Almost all the criticism this mother smeared on was ridiculous—clearly not true. It was like she was describing a character in her imagination but not the person who was sitting in front of her. As I got to know this young lady, I saw that she believed what her mother said. She'd heard all these negative things about herself for so long, that's who she believed she was. She thought that's how everyone saw her.

Any time a person pulls you close with compliments and promises, then turns around in the next moment to take advantage of your trust—any degree of manipulation, from small insults to outright abuse—that person is acting like ivy. They want to take the confidence and abilities that are yours and use them for their own gain. People do this all the time— they appear sweet and interested in others' lives, but pout, criticize, withhold love, gossip, and accuse when they don't get their way. They do this for all kinds of reasons—to sexually molest, to mentally oppress, to take money, to get attention, or simply to exercise power over others. People of any age, race, gender, or type of connection (friend, family,

149

work, school, church, sports, or other) could become an ivy person. Even when they are not physically present, the words of ivy people can get tangled in our thoughts and feelings, and we end up confused about our worth.

Ivy people control others emotionally by alternating disapproval with attention. Ivy people control others relationally, limiting who can be in their lives. Ivy people control others physically, requiring they spend time how, where, and when they dictate. Ivy people use comparison as a scare tactic. Those they control never feel good enough, because ivy people tell them they are not.

In the story of Sarai and Hagar, we see ivy in action. (This story in Genesis 16 takes place before God has changed their names to Abraham and Sarah; that happens later as part of His special Covenant promises.) Sarai is understandably upset—she's past childbearing years and hasn't been able to have a child. She doesn't like the circumstances or timeline that God allowed, so she comes up with a plan to "fix" how God had "failed" her. "Have a baby with my handmaid, then I'll be happy," she suggested to Abram. Even though they didn't have a full understanding of the moral standard God would clarify in the Law He later gave to Moses, they knew about God's holiness. It had been taught from generation to generation. She knew better than to suggest what she did.

There are all kinds of problems with Sarai's suggestion. First, from the beginning, God's pattern and intention for marriage was one woman and one man bound together as a supportive team for life (Genesis 2, Mark 10:6-9, Hebrews 13:4). Any mix-up of God's plan has ramifications that affect the adults, their children, and the whole community—still does. I'm not saying God can't work in imperfect circumstances—I'm saying marriage is serious. Sarai should have considered that rebelling against God's entire social structure wasn't a healthy way to cure her sadness. As is usually the case with any plan we concoct outside of God's counsel and timing, Sarai wasn't thinking long-term. She wanted what she wanted at that moment, and she didn't think about long-term challenges or complications of her plan.

As soon as Hagar got pregnant, she started treating Sarai with contempt. We don't know exactly what that means, but use your imagination. For years, this young Egyptian had been a servant, helping with meals, baths, fetching anything Sarai wanted, doing her every wish. She may not have wanted to get pregnant with Abram's child, but she didn't have a say over her own future. Sarai controlled it. So when she got pregnant, she may have rubbed it in—perhaps acted superior because she got pregnant and Sarai couldn't. Maybe she stopped doing the jobs Sarai told her to do and said, "I can't. I'm pregnant."

Whatever was said and done, Sarai didn't like how Hagar was treating her and she complained to Abram. Did you catch that she totally blamed him for all of it? She made herself out to be the generous, good one in the story—"I gave you my handmaid so we could have a family. Now you and she are ganging up on me with all the baby talk." The sleeping around was *her* idea. No one else may have thought of it. *She* caused the problem, but she wanted everyone else to take the blame. In the end, she abused Hagar to the point that she fled. An angel urged Hagar to return, but the household struggled with emotional toxicity from then on—the servants, Abram and Sarai, and the brothers Ishmael and Isaac all let comparison and jealousy control their thoughts and decisions lifelong. The world still deals with the fight between the descendants of Ishmael and Isaac.

If Sarai had waited a few more years without interfering with God's timeline, she would have welcomed her miracle baby without hurting Hagar. Instead, by carrying out her idea, she messed with Hagar's life, allowed young Ishmael to grow up in a manipulative household, and complicated life for her baby Isaac before he was ever born. She got what she wanted and found it wasn't at all what she wanted.

So many people are like Sarai. They can't wait for God to work. They come up with ideas of things that will make them happy, then blame others for the consequences after *they* arranged the circumstances they wanted. One difficulty in dealing with ivy people is that, by the time we recognize they are ivy people, we are usually close to them. They may be family members from whom we cannot distance ourselves. They may be friends we care about very much. We can't always cut off the ivy—but we can live in relationships with ivy people without being entangled by their accusations and control.

Our time in this book is limited, but I wanted to at least start the conversation about ivy, because so many people are manipulated into believing they aren't capable and beautiful by people who do not have the right to decide that. This may be an area where you need professional guidance to heal, but here are some starting points to loosen the grip of ivy. In this part, we will talk about a few of them in detail.

1. Consider the story of the ivy person.
2. Recognize what reproach is, and refuse to let it in.
3. Uproot the power of people's words.
4. Enjoy a growing relationship with God.
5. Pray for wisdom.
6. Surround yourself with oaks.

Consider the story of the ivy person.

Having a story of past dysfunction ***does not*** excuse the mistreatment of other human beings. Injustice is never right, and God has strong things to say about how He will judge those who hurt others and never repent. However, knowing the stories of ivy people can help us find perspective. When we can admit that ivy people are hurting and need care, it helps us separate ourselves from their control. Admitting that ivy people are not perfect gives us a healthy view of these individuals, rather than being told how we should feel.

One of the most unusual experiences I've had with an ivy person was at a job where I served as a temp worker. My boss asked me to teach a training. I put a lot of time into preparing, but after the event was over, as my team was debriefing, a coworker remarked how the participants and bosses thought my presentation was ridiculous. Her words were like a slap in the face from out of nowhere. What she said was not true. I knew that. But hearing her words spoken out loud was super hurtful. A few days later, in passing, she shared a little of her story—what her childhood was like with an extremely abusive alcoholic mother. Even though I already knew not to hold onto her critical words too tightly, they definitely impacted me. After hearing her background, though, I understood her more. Knowing her story gave me tremendous compassion for her.

Giving in to ivy people's aggression and accusations does not make them happy or make them feel better. If an ivy person's need for control stems from past abuse, the only thing that will lead to true, lasting peace is dealing with the past—*not* sucking life out of another person. If you allow the ivy person to control you, he or she will require more after you've given all you can. Then the world has two broken

153

people. Another person's wholeness can never result from your efforts to make them happy. Wholeness comes only from finding forgiveness, identity, and purpose in God's love.

God knows the story of the ivy people in your life. He knows why they are so desperate (and, at times, twisted) about receiving and giving love. God wants to reach them, but you do not have to be the sacrifice on the altar of their lives. If you struggle in this area, consider visiting with a Christian counselor even if the ivy person in your life will not.

My guess is that you know some ivy people. Ivy people subconsciously prefer to hold you back, not set you free to live for God. But God doesn't make you stay stuck to the ivy—that's not a requirement to please Him (though the ivy people may have told you it is). In fact, staying stuck to them may keep you from hearing the truth God wants you to hear about your worth in His eyes.

"For am I now seeking the approval of man, or of God? Or am I trying to please man? If I were still trying to please man, I would not be a servant of Christ." Galatians 1:10

You are not responsible to make any person happy or give him or her attention or control, no matter how much you are begged for it. Jesus says you are not a condemned and unworthy person. He says you are loved. I pray you will believe that and that His love will give you courage and wisdom to stop ivy people from controlling you.

CHAPTER 21
Giving People Too Much Power
Drain the power out of what's draining you.

And Haman went out that day joyful and glad of heart. But when Haman saw Mordecai in the king's gate, that he neither rose nor trembled before him, he was filled with wrath against Mordecai. Nevertheless, Haman restrained himself and went home, and he sent and brought his friends and his wife Zeresh. And Haman recounted to them the splendor of his riches, the number of his sons, all the promotions with which the king had honored him, and how he had advanced him above the officials and the servants of the king. Then Haman said, "Even Queen Esther let no one but me come with the king to the feast she prepared. And tomorrow also I am invited by her together with the king. Yet all this is worth nothing to me, so long as I see Mordecai the Jew sitting at the king's gate." Then his wife Zeresh and all his friends said to him, "Let a gallows fifty cubits high be made, and in the morning tell the king to have Mordecai hanged upon it. Then go joyfully with the king to the feast." This idea pleased Haman, and he had the gallows made....

The king again said to Esther, "What is your wish, Queen Esther? It shall be granted you. And what is your request? Even to the half of my kingdom, it shall be fulfilled." Then Queen Esther answered, "If I have found favor in your sight, O king, and if it please the king, let my life be granted me for my wish, and my people for my request. For we have been sold, I and my people, to be destroyed, to be killed, and to be annihilated. If we

155

had been sold merely as slaves, men and women, I would have been silent, for our affliction is not to be compared with the loss to the king." Then King Ahasuerus said to Queen Esther, "Who is he, and where is he, who has dared to do this?" And Esther said, "A foe and enemy! This wicked Haman!" Then Haman was terrified before the king and the queen.

And the king arose in his wrath from the wine-drinking and went into the palace garden, but Haman stayed to beg for his life from Queen Esther, for he saw that harm was determined against him by the king. And the king returned from the palace garden to the place where they were drinking wine, as Haman was falling on the couch where Esther was. And the king said, "Will he even assault the queen in my presence, in my own house?" As the word left the mouth of the king, they covered Haman's face. Then Harbona, one of the eunuchs in attendance on the king, said, "Moreover, the gallows that Haman has prepared for Mordecai, whose word saved the king, is standing at Haman's house, fifty cubits high." And the king said, "Hang him on that." So they hanged Haman on the gallows that he had prepared for Mordecai.

Esther 5:9-14, 7:2-10

One of the boys I had a crush on at church camp had a sister who became a close friend. They lived only a half hour away, so we ended up doing lots of fun things together—school dances, sleepovers, and summer fair pageants. My friend was beautiful and incredibly talented—she made her own dresses for the pageants and knew how to speak well in front of a crowd. I really admired her, and it was hard for me not to feel inferior when we were together. I felt unstylish, unattractive, and unaccomplished compared to her. She didn't say or do anything to make me feel that way. I chose to put her on a pedestal. And I always let her decide what we'd do or talk about.

But my friend had some secrets I didn't know until later. She struggled with bulimia, an eating disorder, to the point of being hospitalized. She also struggled with kleptomania, impulsive stealing. She stole one of my favorite things from me while we roomed together at camp. When it happened, it didn't even cross my mind that she could have been the one who stole it. I couldn't bring her down in my eyes. A few months later, when she took something else from me during a sleepover, it clicked. So here I was admiring my friend to the point of belittling myself and giving into her preferences, but my overwhelming admiration didn't take away her sadness, and it didn't help me become who I was supposed to be.

Admiration isn't wrong, but we have to be careful with it. When we idolize people, our hearts become unbalanced and we start feeling *blah* about ourselves. One common example of this is idolizing celebrities: we don't agree with their character or know much about their private lives but their looks, wealth, and fame make them feel powerful, so we follow them on social media, watch their movies, and get wrapped up in their success—and end up feeling down inside.

157

We have to be careful with admiration because of its unique ability to guide our hearts. There's a fine line between admiration and worship. We can't let a person—because of their popularity or position—control our decisions or feelings about ourselves. Admiration is personally crippling if we conclude our contributions are small and ineffective compared to those we admire.

You can certainly find solid role models. God created us to live in community, and thinking we don't need or can't learn from others is not helpful. But more often, our default is to stop trying because we are intimidated by a person with "power"—whether they have a political position or simply popularity at work, school, or church. We go along with them without saying what we think. We let them unsettle us and we don't become all God wants us to be.

Recognize what reproach is, and refuse to let it in.

One technique ivy people use to keep others under their thumb is treating them with disdain, also called reproach. The Latin meaning of the word "reproach" is *to hold back*. People who treat you with reproach, for whatever warped reason, their intention is to keep your life restricted. Reproach is when someone acts like they are better than another person by ignoring or talking down to them, pointing out their faults, getting others to join in talking about them, or not allowing them to participate. It happens when one person despises another out of jealousy or because they can't control them.

In the story of Esther (what a story—I hope you read it all!), we see a young lady learn to push back against the influence of those who had wealth, prestige, and power over life and death.

Esther, an orphan who had been adopted by her Uncle Mordecai, lived in the kingdom of Persia about 100 years after the Babylonian captivity of the Jews. Although many Jews had returned to resettle the homeland, some still lived where they had been taken. Unexpectedly, Esther was chosen out of a huge parade of women to be the new queen, and she was ushered into an unusual situation: she was the king's wife, but if she approached him without being invited, he could kill her.

The king wasn't the only person in the empire with authority. His second-in-command, Haman, also loved power. He made a law that people had to bow when he passed by. Haman hated Mordecai because he wouldn't bow down to him. Every day, Haman told Mordecai he was a nobody and a rule-breaker. But Mordecai didn't let the reproach in. He wouldn't be controlled by Haman. He wouldn't bow to anyone but Almighty God. So Haman expanded his disdain from Mordecai to all Jewish people. He made a new law that on a set day, everyone could attack the Jews in the area, kill them, and take their stuff. That's what people in positions of power sometimes do—they make threats against the security of people they're actually responsible for keeping safe.

So Esther needed to approach the king and explain Haman's intentions. She had to come clean that she was a Jew. She alone was in a position to ask the king for protection for her people. She didn't have the courage to do this on her own—she needed a little nudge from her Uncle Mordecai, who reminded her that God is greater than kings. By personal prayer and asking others to pray over her, she found strength to expose Haman's evil plan, regardless of the outcome. She got to the place where she drained all of Haman's—and the king's—intimidation out of her decision. She decided she'd rather die for speaking up than live as a coward.

Esther chose to honor God over humans. She risked her life to prevent Haman from having the power he wanted. When she spoke up, her courage literally multiplied. Other royal attendants joined in reporting Haman's unsavory activities to the king. It often happens that if we find courage to remove an unsafe person's power over us, we will inspire others to do the same. Because of Esther's request, the king agreed to a law that said the Jews could protect themselves if Haman's cronies attacked them, and they were saved.

Esther's story shows us that God is bigger than those who treat us with reproach. In the end, she didn't lose her life. Haman did. Standing up to powerful people doesn't always result in deliverance as dramatic as this. But I hope you can see that pleasing God is more important than pleasing people and that God can be trusted more than powerful people.

Esther didn't know what would happen when she went to the king. Her goal wasn't Haman's death. Her goal was to speak up for her people. Likewise, our goal as we deal with ivy people isn't the eradication of our enemies—it's the introduction of courage into our daily lives, the guts to speak the truth about God, even if it results in ridicule. We don't have to be afraid of rejection because we are loved by Him. In fact, Jesus promised that we will be blessed if we are persecuted for doing right (Matthew 5:10-12).

You are God's priceless treasure that He paid for at the high expense of His Son's life. He does not want you to allow yourself to be mistreated and told you are worthless. It is time to stand up to the Hamans in your life. If needed, make an action plan like Esther did and ask others to stand with you. Drain the intimidation. Check whom you are admiring. Find strength to say what needs to be said. It's time for the garden of your life to be ivy free.

CHECKING YOUR THOUGHT PATTERNS

We may not realize we have been listening to others' wounding words—or a self-destructive internal narrative—until it consumes our thought life. Watch for these hurtful ways of thinking as you learn to let go of comparison.

- Hypocrisy- Hypocrisy is holding other people to a standard we cannot and do not want to live up to ourselves. It is expecting perfection of people so we have an excuse to criticize them.

- Fear of people's opinions- We spend time and energy worrying what people think of us and trying to please strangers. Valuing people's opinions over God's can actually keep us from doing what He wants.

- Greed/love of money- Humans tend to measure worth by the amount of stuff we have and the brands we wear. It's completely senseless, but we give power to tags to make us feel special. When money is the main thing that makes us feel validated, we need a heart check.

- Never enough- Ivy people say you need to do or give more. You may tell yourself your accomplishments should be more. The right thoughts and friends influence you to draw close to the Lord and do what He created you to do, not feel worse about your abilities.

CHAPTER 22
The Judgy Weeds

Others' judgmental words do not change Jesus' decision to love us.

Joseph, being seventeen years old, was pasturing the flock with his brothers.... And Joseph brought a bad report of them to their father. Now Israel [Jacob] loved Joseph more than any other of his sons, because he was the son of his old age. And he made him a robe of many colors. But when his brothers saw that their father loved him more than all his brothers, they hated him and could not speak peacefully to him.

They saw him from afar, and before he came near to them they conspired against him to kill him. They said to one another, "Here comes this dreamer. Come now, let us kill him and throw him into one of the pits. Then we will say that a fierce animal has devoured him, and we will see what will become of his dreams." ....And Reuben said to them, "Shed no blood; throw him into this pit here in the wilderness, but do not lay a hand on him"— that he might rescue him out of their hand to restore him to his father. So when Joseph came to his brothers, they stripped him of his robe, the robe of many colors.... And they took him and threw him into a pit....

Then they sat down to eat. And looking up they saw a caravan of Ishmaelites coming from Gilead, with their camels bearing gum, balm, and myrrh, on their way to carry it down to Egypt. Then Judah said to his brothers, "What profit is it if we kill our brother and conceal his blood? Come, let us sell him to the Ishmaelites, and let not our hand be upon him, for he is our brother, our own flesh." And his brothers listened to him.

Genesis 27:2-4, 18-27

"All the boys call me 'Snout,'" my daughter with an adorable nose told me one afternoon halfway through her freshman year.

My mom's first name is Rolinda, after a beautiful flower. All her life, she has gone by her middle name because kids called her "Roll-y Poll-y Rolinda" in elementary school.

People think they're so clever. Really, they're just cruel. It's bad enough when acquaintances do it. What do you do when it's family?

In Joseph's family, it was obvious he was his father Jacob's favorite son—the colorful robe Jacob gave him wasn't the only sign. So when Joseph told his family about the dreams he had of them bowing to him—perhaps in childish immaturity, perhaps in a boastful way—his brothers, who were already jealous, began to despise him. When he told Jacob they were not doing a good job in the fields, that was the last straw. They sold him to some slave traders.

Joseph endured human trafficking, being accused of attacking his master's wife when he didn't (see Genesis 39:6-18), and waiting years to get out of prison. For every undeserved problem that happened to him, he responded with obedience to God. Every time someone said he was something he wasn't, instead of moping or becoming bitter about the injustice, he fixed his eyes on doing his job. He didn't argue with people. He didn't defend himself. He didn't act out or become rebellious. He worked according to his character and trusted the truth to come out. And when the time came for vindication, he didn't rub it in.

During the famine, when Joseph rescued his brothers (about 13 years after being sold as a slave), he praised God for the steps his life had taken. He could have viewed his trauma

163

as horrific—it was—but he saw God's hand in it, and that gave him the ability to forgive and fulfill his purpose.

> "And he said, 'I am your brother, Joseph, whom you sold into Egypt. And now do not be distressed or angry with yourselves because you sold me here, for God sent me before you to preserve life.... So it was not you who sent me here, but God.'"
> Genesis 45:4-8

Joseph had figured out early that he answered to God for his choices. He could trust God to use him where he was, regardless of others' opinions toward him. Jesus handled criticism in a similar way. He didn't loudly stand up for Himself and argue with the world's opinion. He also didn't hold onto it as if it were remotely true. People's opinions did not sway His focus. He was called every name from devil to King of the Jews. People said, "Nothing good comes from Nazareth." Their words didn't stop Him. Jesus didn't wait for the crowd's approval to start God's work, and He didn't stop doing what God wanted when the crowd didn't like it.

Let's be honest, we can be a little judgy toward others, too. With a tiny bit of information, we make huge pronouncements about another person's worth. We sometimes say super smart-aleck criticisms that are completely wrong. We think we are clever, but maybe we are a little... cruel. ***Do we spend more time gossiping about people than getting to know them?***

A few years ago as I tucked my third-grade daughter into bed, she told me some girls at school teamed up and made jokes about her hair and personality. She admitted she really didn't want these girls for friends, but she couldn't shake what they said. At age 8, she asked a profound question: "Why do I concentrate on what they say, when I have good friends who say sweet things about me, like, 'Your hair is so soft'?"

At 8 years old, she knew the difference between trustworthy and untrustworthy commentary. Yet she wanted a reminder of her place as God's child. Tomorrow, she will need another reminder, and I will, too. Because every day people feel it necessary to comment on the value and abilities of those they don't know.

Unless God helps us get out of the habit, we judge strangers, too. One area of judgment may be an area where we desire to be recognized. A pastor friend once said, "It is a temptation to be hyper-critical of those who are using a gift we have but are not using." This is so true. Ask God for opportunities to serve, and guard your heart from jealousy.

Sometimes you get the sense that others are judging you. If that judgment is in an area where you struggle, you may assume a lot more judgment than is actually there. In fact, almost all of the time, we assume others' judgment is much more severe than it is. But, for the sake of example, let's say some girl's judgment of you is severe and she spreads gossip around like the coronavirus. Unless her concerns are voiced to God as a prayer on your behalf, God's not taking them into consideration. Oh, He hears our sin of judgment, gossip, and complaining about one another. But He's not depending on the counsel of humans who are tangled up in jealousy to make His decision how He feels about you. To be clear: someone else's sin of judging you doesn't bring you condemnation; it reveals something about *her* heart.

God's idea of all you will become is not based on another person's opinion of you. God's love is based on a decision He made before He spoke light into existence. He chose you twice: He designed your unique face, body, and personality,

and He decided to give the life of His Son in exchange for your missteps, to buy you back from the punishment our choices deserve. He invites you to belong. He wants you at His party.

FILTERING CRITICISM

Use these questions to weigh opinions you hear—and say:

- Is the statement true? Is it kind?
- Is the opinion based on an accurate understanding of the person, or is one scenario being taken out of context?
- Is the judgment biased because of jealousy or an opposite point of view?
- Is the conversation pure and useful? Does it lead the hearers to God?
- Does the thought include love and forgiveness?
- Do they/I know all the facts?

We don't realize that wanting to make people happy could be disobedience to God. Sometimes it's not, but many times trying to avoid criticism by appeasing people leads us to cross a line. It makes us compromise our convictions or stay silent when we should stand up. It makes us alter our personality—and for what? To please people who may decide they still don't "like" us or that we have to keep doing what they want to maintain their approval?

As long as humans live and breathe, we will deal with unsolicited advice and outlandish name calling. Just because they say those words doesn't mean they are true. Joseph didn't listen to human opinion to decide whether he had a role in the world or not. He made a difference even when he'd been talked about. You can, too.

Don't give away your worth to the creeping ivy or ignore Jesus's sacrifice by thinking that you are only what people say you are. Others' judgy words do not change your value or abilities. So go ahead—be all God created you to be. No one's opinion can stop that—unless you let it.

UPROOT THE POWER OF PEOPLE'S WORDS

Are words like these filling your mind?

Can't	Unpopular	Untalented
Lazy	Weak	Sick
Negative	Ugly	Bad
Fat	Stupid	Unforgivable

You may not be able to control the words that come out of others' mouths, but you can uproot their power. Your Creator decided on your hair and nose, your body type and talents. He celebrates in your immeasurable beauty. You are a reflection of His creative work and incomparable glory.

The words above are not the words your Heavenly Father uses to describe people He made and wants to save! So we must get out of the habit of using them to describe ourselves or others. If we repeat words and phrases that directly oppose what Scripture says about our worth and place, we are believing the thoughts of people and our Enemy over God's.

Stand up and decide that you believe God's words. With agony and shed blood, He paid for the right to call us by this identity:

Forgiven	Contributing	Beautiful
Exchanged	Insightful	Healthy
Able	Gifted	Strong
Chosen	Beloved	Kind

CHAPTER 23
At the Root of Complaining
If you can't say anything nice, check to see what's going on inside.

From Mount Hor they set out by the way to the Red Sea, to go around the land of Edom. And the people became impatient on the way. And the people spoke against God and against Moses, "Why have you brought us up out of Egypt to die in the wilderness? For there is no food and no water, and we loathe this worthless food." Then the Lord sent fiery serpents among the people, and they bit the people, so that many people of Israel died. And the people came to Moses and said, "We have sinned, for we have spoken against the Lord and against you. Pray to the Lord, that he take away the serpents from us." So Moses prayed for the people. And the Lord said to Moses, "Make a fiery serpent and set it on a pole, and everyone who is bitten, when he sees it, shall live." So Moses made a bronze serpent and set it on a pole. And if a serpent bit anyone, he would look at the bronze serpent and live.

Numbers 21:4-9

One night, my oldest and my youngest were meeting up with me for dinner after exercise class. We don't do this every week, so I was looking forward to treating them. I picked a nice pizza place close to the class and texted them the location. When they finished working out and saw where I'd picked, one asked, "Can I get anything lactose free?" and the other said, "Why are we going there?" They were getting hot, free food—I couldn't understand why they didn't want what I picked—until I tried their class the next week. At the end of an hour of barre, you need a shower and a stretcher, not a pizza! I complain a lot, too. I wonder if it's because we have so much. Subtly, a message has wormed its way into our thinking: we deserve whatever we want when we want it, and those who withhold it, delay it, or make us work for it are treating us unfairly.

Our culture isn't the only one that struggles with complaining. Remember Joseph from our last chapter? During the seven-year famine, he distributed the grain Egypt had stored up to feed hungry people in the whole region. His family (father Jacob and 11 brothers, 1 sister, and their families) moved close to him. They intended to return to the land that God had promised after the famine, but they stayed for many generations because they settled into land, homes, and jobs there. In Egypt, Joseph's family was a minority race. Within a couple of generations, the royal line in Egypt forgot about how Joseph made their king richer and saved the country with the storehouses of grain. I don't know how they could forget that, but they did. The Egyptian king, called Pharaoh, decided he wanted to build a more advanced country than those around him. He needed laborers to build houses, waterways, and monuments. He noticed how numerous, talented, and physically strong the Hebrews were. He didn't want them to take over his country, but he also did not want them to leave the country, so he enslaved them to do his work. They were slaves for generations.

The work the Hebrews did was back-breaking. They had food and homes, but they were made fun of and mistreated. They prayed for help. When God told Moses it was time for deliverance, He said, "I have surely seen the affliction of my people who are in Egypt and have heard their cry because of their taskmasters. I know their sufferings, and I have come down to deliver them out of the hand of the Egyptians and to bring them up out of that land to a good and broad land, a land flowing with milk and honey" (Exodus 3:7-8).

The story of the Israelites' deliverance from a brutal Egyptian Pharaoh (Exodus 14:21-31) is remarkable: the Red Sea parted and they (nearly a million people) walked across on a dry path—not a muddy river bottom—with high walls of water on both sides. Then God twisted the wheels of Pharaoh's army's chariots, and the walls of water crashed over them. God clearly led the steps of His people with a pillar of cloud by day and fire by night. God caused their clothes and shoes not to wear out for 40 years. They watched the power of God literally working for them. But His provision wasn't enough to keep them from complaining. After all the glorious displays of God's might, the Hebrews wished they hadn't left Egypt. Why? They didn't like the food.

For much of the journey, the Hebrews traveled in a desert area. Food and water were scarce. God fed the people with wafers of bread that fell from the sky, called manna, and provided water from streams and even rocks. They had everything they needed. The journey was supposed to take only a couple months. God had told them the new place they were to live and how they were going to take over their new

170

homeland. But when scouts saw super tall, strong people living in this area, they didn't believe God's deliverance plan was enough (see Exodus 23:27-29), so they cowered and continued to wander in the desert.

Forty-ish days turned into forty years. The people got restless. They didn't want to listen to God and Moses any longer. They got so angry with God's plan and provision, they said, "Would that we had died by the hand of the Lord in the land of Egypt, when we sat by the meat pots and ate bread to the full, for you have brought us out into this wilderness to kill this whole assembly with hunger" (Exodus 16:3). They forgot the hardships and abuse of Egypt and glamorized their captors, wishing to be back in their old situation. Why? They didn't like the food.

> "He then told them, 'Watch out and be on guard against all greed because one's life is not in the abundance of his possessions.'"
> Luke 12:15 (HCSB)

The Israelites' complaining resulted in a tragic turn: fiery serpents bit and killed some of them. To reverse the work of the serpents, God had Moses fashion a bronze snake on a pole—not for them to worship as an idol or good luck charm, but as an act of faith and a means of rescue. The sculpture was both a picture of the death the Israelites' words were bringing upon themselves and a foreshadowing that the Messiah would die on a raised pole. The healing was from God, through faith in His immeasurable power, not from the pole. Holding up the power of God in front of their complaining was meant to lead to repentance—truly being sorry they complained about the provision of God.

171

Here's the thing about complaining: we will never stop if we don't figure out what's causing it. Complaining starts when we compare our current circumstances to what we wish they were. We hold our lives up against what others have and decide that what we have is not enough. So we grumble. We don't like the rules. We don't like the clothes. We don't like the food. We grumble against those who make the rules, who give us what we have, and who make the food. We're convinced we deserve more—stuff, attention, all of it.

Jesus taught a new perspective on accumulation and contentment. He explained that life doesn't come from having stuff. If life came from them, our desperation for them would be understandable. But if they are simply *part* of life and not life itself, then we can accept when situations or plans change. We can eat manna without complaining.

Paul taught a new perspective about complaining, too. He said we can learn to respond to things that make us feel anxious or let down with prayer and thankfulness. This response doesn't negate the trials of life. It is the most constructive way to cope with them—reminding ourselves that our Creator and loving Father wants to meet the needs of our heart and life.

We may need to have a conversation with a friend about something that is wrong. We are certainly allowed to say how we feel. What we want to watch for is that line between voicing an occasional genuine concern and becoming a complainer. The habit of complaining is like ivy—it starts in one little spot then quickly takes over other areas. We don't want it to become our only point of view or primary form of communication. The great news is, we can cultivate contentment. We can learn to ask, "What is God up to?" instead of "**What if** everything was better?"

WHAT ARE WHAT-IFS?

What-ifs are questions we ask ourselves that compare our real circumstances to impossibly perfect ones—then we complain that life isn't like that. Here are some tips to help you recognize ivy thought patterns:

- What-ifs usually dwell on the past. They make us grovel in regret rather than making wise decisions now.

- What-ifs focus on what's gone wrong.

- What-ifs almost always center around having more money, fame, or some other thing we think would make life easier.

- What-ifs lead us to doubt God's love and leading.

- What-ifs question God's ability to take us from where we are right now to where He wants us to go.

- What-ifs trigger comparison.

Change your what-ifs to these questions:

- What will God do through this?

- How will He show Himself in my weakness, brokenness, and loss? How might it be better for me than ease?

- Have I thanked Him for anything today?

Take a look inside—where is your complaining coming from? Are you afraid God has forgotten you? Do you feel unimportant and unloved? Is your current trial harder than you ever dreamed? Do you want more pretty stuff? The root of our complaining is usually a mix of lots of reasons.

Like Moses did with the serpent on the pole, holding Jesus up in front of every comparison keeps us from having a grumbling heart. Every sunrise, meal, breath, kindness and comfort is from His hand. Together, let's ask God to help us be content in the middle of our manna moments.

WHAT IF SOMETHING GOES WRONG?

When plans change or the world comes to a grinding halt like it did with the coronavirus, it's hard not to be disappointed and ask, "God, why did you let this happen?" It can feel like God is mean or insensitive. It can feel like your life is ruined. I've been there—we lost two babies during pregnancy, lost almost half the equity in our home during the economic downturn in 2008, and, like everyone, had many plans cancelled because of COVID-19. Again and again, I tried getting books published and with every no, I wrestled with His call. Everyone experiences heartbreaking loss and delays. Through the years, God has shown me that nothing can stop the work He does in hearts and that accomplishment is a matter of perspective.

Our culture has indoctrinated us into believing that the greatest pillars of life are security, success, and prosperity. But life isn't ruined when these things stop. What if the relentless pursuit of fame, fortune, and safety are the things distracting our focus and stalling our call? If the greatest gain in life is knowing Jesus and our greatest goal is honoring Him, don't be so quick to write off what He may be teaching through disappointment. Just because an experience is hard doesn't mean it isn't worthwhile. Sometimes loss leads to hearing Him better than gain. Sometimes pruning leads to more fruitfulness. Ask Him for growth and wisdom through the ups and downs of life.

In the winter, the temperatures cause sap to slow inside a tree. If a freeze settles on its flowers in the spring, the blossoms let loose and flutter away. But cold weather doesn't kill trees. Though the growth is almost indiscernible, the tree is still thriving. In fact, without wind and changes in seasons, trees don't push their roots deeper. If you face an unexpected disappointment, know that God will never leave you or forsake you. He knows what is going on, and He knows what will happen in and through you because of it.

CHAPTER 24
Recognizing Idols
Anything that competes with God's place is an idol.

After this I heard what seemed to be the loud voice
of a great multitude in heaven, crying out, "Hallelujah!
Salvation and glory and power belong to our God, for
his judgments are true and just; for he has judged the
great prostitute who corrupted the earth with her
immorality...."

And the twenty-four elders and the four living
creatures fell down and worshiped God who was seated
on the throne, saying, "Amen. Hallelujah!" And from the
throne came a voice saying, "Praise our God, all you his
servants...."

Then I heard what seemed to be the voice of a great
multitude, like the roar of many waters and like the
sound of mighty peals of thunder, crying out, "Hallelujah!
For the Lord our God the Almighty reigns. Let us rejoice
and exult and give him the glory, for the marriage of the
Lamb has come, and his Bride has made herself ready....

And the angel said to me, "Write this: Blessed are
those who are invited to the marriage supper of the
Lamb...." Then I saw heaven opened, and behold, a white
horse! The one sitting on it is called Faithful and True,
and in righteousness he judges and makes war. His eyes
are like a flame of fire, and on his head are many
diadems, and he has a name written that no one knows
but himself. He is clothed in a robe dipped in blood, and
the name by which he is called is The Word of God.... On
his robe and on his thigh he has a name written, King of
kings and Lord of lords.

Revelation 19:1-16

I remember the first time I saw pot. I was 15. My brother was a year older. His substance abuse started at a young age. He started with using dip (tobacco). Then cigarettes. Then drinking. Heavily. He'd ask me to clean up his vomit when he'd had too much. When my brother pulled out a zip-top baggie of weed one day, I didn't want him to start down that road. I didn't know he already was. Shaking, I grabbed the bag, ran to the toilet, and tried to spill the contents into the water. He chased me, snatched the bag, screamed at me, then ran out of the house. In coming years, he went on to use cocaine, heroin, and acid, whatever he could get his hands on. He was close to death several times.

He stopped using drugs and settled in to decades of drinking. When he stopped drinking, he took pills. Then he started drinking again—with pot and pills. At the end of his life, he saw things that weren't there and heard people who weren't speaking. Then he died two months before turning 50. My parents are hard-working and generous people. They modeled loving and trusting Jesus. Before Bible studies and podcasts were cool, before worship music was even really a thing, they found Christian resources to help us and prayed with us every day. They taught us that drinking and drugs would ruin our lives. I heard my brother say, "They don't know anything about this. I can stop whenever I want, and what I do is not hurting anyone." He wasn't right about that—he couldn't stop, and it hurt all of us every day, every year for his whole life, and still hurts now that he's gone. We loved him, but we could not control his cravings or keep him from hurting himself or others.

For me, this real life agony is a picture of all of us with our Heavenly Father. Here we are, thinking we are so in control, that we are above consequences and more genius than the Maker of the Universe. We do what we want to do, while our loving Father is calling to us, trying to teach us, speak to us, and give blessings to us. We resist the grace and truth He wants to pour into our lives, choosing instead our baggie, our bottle, our temporary partner, our craving. We insist on our independence. We say what we do is no big deal—everyone's doing it. And then...it eats us alive.

So far in this part, we have talked about people and thought patterns that grow and overtake us like ivy. Now let's talk about ivy pursuits—possessions, hobbies, and habits we are attached to. How we start our little (and big) areas of rebellion. What gets us to the place where we are willing to cross that line *just this once?*

"Just this once" can turn into, "I can't live without it."

I mean, nobody ever looked at a pill and said, "Gee, I hope this will help me become a raging abuser with no home," or "Wow, I can't wait to slam my car into an innocent child while I'm under the influence." Nobody ever flirted with a friend, whispered a lie, or took a little something at work or a store and planned on getting so wrapped up or losing so big. So what gets us to that point where we are willing to risk our lives, relationships, jobs, homes, and careers for our insatiable desires? Why do the very things our Father has asked us not to do with our life, energy, money, and time? We embrace the lies of the Enemy and cannot get them out of our head.

When we pursue something outside God's counsel, we make the decision to put that thing, person, or pursuit in the place of God—trusting it to help us somehow more than obeying God would. Anything that excessively absorbs our attention becomes an object of worship. And anything that inches its way into the place of God in our lives is an idol.

I'm not saying if you puff a vape or make a mistake one time, you'll be a lifelong addict. It is also possible to never touch anything addictive and still be fully guilty of idolatry. What we have to ask ourselves is this: **what is driving your heart?** Why do you want to try what you want to try—even if it is only once? Watch for over-attachment—even if it is to "innocent" things.

We don't like to think of our areas of resistance as idolatry. "I don't worship statues. It's only a show. It's just a few more minutes on my phone. It's casual. It's not immoral." But a tell-tale sign that something is an idol is our refusal to give it up or the lengths we go to hide it.

What we choose to chase reveals what we believe about the power of those pursuits and the power of God.

What do you prefer spending your time doing when no one else is around? Does it tick you off if someone suggests slowing down or stopping your habit, or that it is taking you down the wrong road? Do you worry you won't have time or money for it today? Does the habit sway your emotions? Do you give it unreasonable amounts of time? If others started going after this thing the way you have, would you say they're going overboard? Yet if someone wants to warn us, we often think, "Don't you dare confront me." Be careful: in nature, the things that get attached to other living organisms are parasites. Unhealthy relationships aren't the only thing that works like ivy to drain us of our vibrant lives. Other stuff can, too—hobbies, habits, material goods, and ways of responding to circumstances and people. It's true not everything we want is immoral, but if the *way* we want it has become offensive to God, it's time to exercise self-control and say no.

> "Mankind...did not repent of the works of their hands nor give up worshiping demons and idols of gold and silver and bronze and stone and wood, which cannot see or hear or walk, nor did they repent of their murders or their sorceries or their sexual immorality or their thefts."
> Revelation 9:20-21

We believe things, people, and pursuits will bring us tremendous happiness, but is the happiness real? For example, we think wealth will bring us status, but then people may only know us for what we own and not the person we are. We may think the intimacy of lover after lover will cure our insecurity, but our body and mind will ping anxiety overload with that many relationships in rapid succession. We assume that time on our phones will make us a star in our circle and fear that if we're not on it, we'll miss something—but we feel worse after giving hours to the screen. Cars wear out. Fashion trends end. Vacations don't go as planned. Bodies get sick. Without realizing it, we're handing our hope over to things that don't work, don't last, and end up hurting.

What can we do when we realize that something is taking up too much room in our heart? Put God back in His rightful place, where other things have crept in. Cultivate the right view of God by studying His Word. The more clearly we see His love and power, the more we will hate and run from the

179

things that are rebellion against Him. The more clearly we see sin for what it is, the more we will be drawn to God and run to Him. Until we are disgusted by sin, though, we will be enamored by it.

Revelation 18 is an honest description of the state of the world and the state of our hearts if we are not careful to guard them. It describes the things that people have loved and pursued more than God. Many of the things listed are not immoral in and of themselves—how can cinnamon be evil (Revelation 18:13)? Scripture is not preaching against spices. It is making a point about how our hearts latch onto luxuries. God is communicating that when human beings treasure anything more than Him—no matter how innocent a product or plan might be—that passion moves us to places we didn't anticipate. The things the world system offers can grow into idols. We refuse to live without them.

If "everybody's doing it" is your excuse to keep doing it, take an honest look at what **it** is doing to your life.

All of us are guilty of loving position and possessions more than the living God. Any sin is an offense to God, a stench. Any sin breaks His heart and damages our lives and relationships. We protect sin, excuse it, hide it, and refuse to talk about it. But God wants us to see that sin is keeping us first from Him, then from one another—and also from becoming all we can be. He wants us to stop cherishing sin and learn to enjoy obedience.

Revelation 18 is not where the story ends. Revelation 19 teaches us how to get rid of idolatry in our hearts: open your eyes to see the glory of God. When we highly value Him, the

Enemy cannot deceive us any longer. Ivy people, pursuits, and thought patterns can bind us no longer. The Knight on the white horse we have been waiting for will ride in with final victory over delusion.

The word *hallelujah*, which means "God be praised," is used in only one place in the Bible—right here in Revelation 19, when sin and idolatry are destroyed and thrown into hell forever. It is sung three times, the sign of completion, by the crowds of God's people. One day, everyone will kneel and declare that Jesus is inarguably the Faithful and True Savior. Before that moment, though, every time we as believers "see" His sovereignty and act on it—every time we choose Him over self-centered, self-promoting activities and attitudes— our lives are saying, "Hallelujah."

If idolatry is the adoration of people and things, then the opposite of idolatry is worship of the only God. Learning to worship Him takes practice and discipline, constant reminders that He is greater and we are less. It means we intentionally decide that He is better, wiser, and worthier than anyone, anything, or any thought.

Ultimately, we will never overcome comparison until we learn to worship Him. Without worship, we tend to push ourselves up to the throne where He alone belongs. If He is seated there, we see that God Himself is the source of all we need, the answer to our need for relief, healing, and validation. Then we change what we're going after.

The great hymn "Amazing Grace" reminds us: "I once was lost, but now am found; T'was blind but now I see." Now that we see ivy people, pursuits, and thought patterns for what they are, we can make the better choice—to know Jesus and His love.

THE TEMPTATION TO REBEL AFTER DISAPPOINTMENT

Any time God, parents, friends, or life leaves us feeling unloved or let down, we grasp for control, fulfillment, and attention. If we don't like what God has allowed, we sometimes tell ourselves stuff like, "God didn't fix that for me. I deserve some happiness, so I'll do what I want. He doesn't care anyway." We proclaim our independence, because that feels like freedom. But if we choose people, pursuits, or thought patterns that oppose God's will, bondage and brokenness are in quick step right behind.

Rebellion is often connected to aimlessness. The thing we rebel with—the action or attitude—has nothing to do with what we're mad about. The loss God allowed (for example, sickness or death of a loved one) is not connected in any way to what we choose to cope with our grief (for example, sexual sin or heavy drinking).

The more we ignore God's Word and do what we want, the less we have clear direction. The more we feel bored, tired, or purposeless, the more we experiment with things to make us feel "alive." If we habitually push God down when He wants to speak, the assertion of our will drowns His voice and we're left to figure life out without Him. Rebellion can never deliver on what it promises. Even in the moment it is bringing pleasure, it is also bringing pain.

The bottom line is, sometimes we just don't want to put Jesus in a place of authority. We don't want Him to come between us and our decisions. Our anger with Him is our excuse for sin, but we need to remember, He is not to blame for our personal decisions, for the decisions of other people, or for the death and decay that exists in the world.

If we can learn to recognize signs and triggers of rebellion against God and practice drawing close to Him even when our emotions don't feel committed, we will protect our hearts and bring Him glory.

"Do not be anxious about anything,
but in everything by prayer and supplication
with thanksgiving let your requests be made
known to God. And the peace of God,
which surpasses all understanding,
will guard your hearts and your minds
in Christ Jesus.
Finally, brothers, whatever is true,
whatever is honorable, whatever is just,
whatever is pure, whatever is lovely,
whatever is commendable, if there is any
excellence, if there is anything worthy of praise,
think about these things."
Philippians 4:6-8

Part 6

LOOKING FOR OAKS

Finding Peace and Purpose

"Now to Him who is able to do above and beyond all
that we ask or think according to the power that works
in us—to Him be glory in the church and in Christ Jesus
to all generations, forever and ever. Amen."
Ephesians 3:20-21, HCSB

Beginning Thoughts

Oak trees are the opposite of ivy. They are strong and provide shelter. While some people, pursuits, and thought patterns creep in and take over, others give life like an oak. Comparison makes lives stagnant, but knowing God loves you makes you bold, confident, and courageous. Now that you've learned to look at comparison with your eyes wide open, let's end our time together filled up with hope. In this part, we look at practical ways to push past comparison because you have found peace and purpose in Christ.

TAKEAWAYS FOR PART 6

- Understanding your personality, natural talents, spiritual gifts, and goals helps you live with purpose.
- You can think about your decisions and plan long-term.
- Get up and go where God leads!

CHAPTER 25

Knowing Who You Are

You learn who you are when you spend time in God's Word.

Jesus, knowing that the Father had given all things into his hands, and that he had come from God and was going back to God, rose from supper. He laid aside his outer garments, and taking a towel, tied it around his waist. Then he poured water into a basin and began to wash the disciples' feet.

John 13:3-5

In middle and high school, I measured my worth in grades and appearance (neither of which I thought was good enough) and felt chronically inferior. If someone said something nice, I immediately discounted it: "I bet she's just saying that to be nice" and other self-rejecting thoughts ran around my head like a bulldozer, digging deep pits of doubt and depression. Even though I believed God loved me, I still feared I wasn't worth loving. I didn't read my Bible much, so I didn't fully understand what His forgiveness meant for my identity. But He heard my prayers and saw my need. And He kept drawing me to Himself.

My freshman year of college, He spoke to my heart about being more serious about paying attention to His Words. I started memorizing Bible verses regularly. Then I read a book called *Search for Significance.* Around that same time, a Bible teacher named Bob Warren came to campus and taught the book of Romans chapter by chapter. Clear and consistent exposure to God's Word changed my life. Through it, God gave me tools and truths to push back against comparison's lies. His Word and His Holy Spirit healed my broken heart— and filled in the ruts dug by negative thought patterns. As an adult woman, at times I've struggled with knowing what to do or feeling like I'm not enough, but His Word won't let me stay there long. His truth has made its way into my thinking and has permanently changed my view of who I am. He has made me certain that I belong to Him.

I've noticed that when people feel uncertain about who they are, they stall. Stalling can take the form of laziness, playing around with sin, and making excuses for not deciding to live for God. Stalling doesn't help us find out who we are; it only feeds the inaccurate notion that we can't do anything to contribute. It's time to stop stalling and start living. It's time to grab the confidence that is yours because of Jesus Christ and live out your new and certain identity.

After working through this book, I hope you clearly see that as a believer in Jesus, you are a ***deeply loved daughter***, a ***forgiven and restored soul***, and a ***person with purpose***. Second Corinthians 5:17 tells us, "Therefore, if anyone is in Christ, he is a new creation. The old has passed away; behold, the new has come." Romans 8:1 explains, "There is therefore now no condemnation for those who are in Christ Jesus." From Jesus, we have received the gift of a second chance—we are released from criticism and given the opportunity to move forward and make a difference in Jesus' name.

But you may still wonder what you are good at—and what specific things you are supposed to do with your time. Learning who you are takes time. That's okay. Gaining skills in *anything* takes time—driving, cooking, drawing, REFIT® (I cannot get those exercise moves down!). The disciplines of our faith and healthy habits are no different. They take practice and effort. But understanding a few key things about ourselves can give us a stronger sense of direction. Let's talk about those briefly.

Personality

One of the big problems with comparison is that each person is vastly different—from backgrounds to natural talents to personality. Many personality theories, such as Enneagram, Meyers-Briggs, and DISC model, help us understand how people are different. It's fun to learn about them, but it's not constructive to negatively compare yourself to people with different personalities. I don't know why humans do this, but we often look at people who land in a different personality quadrant and wonder why we can't be like them—interact with others the way they do.

We were not made to be the same. God did this by His design. If you look at the communication styles and actions of the disciples, you see extroverts and introverts, active and studious, sweet and skeptical, rich and poor, dominant and compliant. In God's heart, there is room for all personalities because He made each one! He values and understands each person. He sees how each one is effective in taking care of people and problems. And He wants each of us! Sure, we can learn skills from each other, but devaluing yourself because your personality isn't like another person's is an inaccurate response to differences.

Don't tell God you can't be used because your personality isn't like *hers*. He already told us nothing is impossible for Him (Mark 10:27). Because of your uniqueness, you can relate to people others can't and have ideas others don't. Often your personality mixed with your natural talents leads you to a job and ministry you are passionate about. The world needs Christ-followers in every vocation and quadrant. God designed your temperament for a purpose—you are essential to building His kingdom.

Character

Character is different from personality. It is the traits you show on a regular basis, the ways you respond in times of ease or trial. We learn some of our character habits in childhood; some are influenced by our personality; and some we choose and learn. Many people think they don't have a choice in how they act—they are a product of their environment—but that is not true. With the help of the Holy Spirit, we can live out

189

character traits that reflect Jesus to others. We can develop more grit and holiness.

Honesty, generosity, patience, and courage are examples of traits you might want to develop. Memorize Bible verses about these strengths. Ask God to grow them in you. Galatians 5:22-23 says we can develop character if we belong to Him. That's good news for the people our lives touch.

Talents & Interests

Everyone is born with abilities they're good at—and things that don't come as easily. (That means you don't have to be great at everything!) Educational psychologists describe our physical brains as having different areas of intelligence. Some people are more athletic, some more verbal, artistic, or musical. Being logical or mathematical, understanding people, remembering well, loving nature, and being a wise decision-maker are skills you may not have realized are talents. When you mix ability with the huge assortment of interests out there, you see genius and creativity, the fingerprints of Creator God on each soul, because we were made in His image.

> "If any of you lacks wisdom, let him ask God, who gives generously to all without reproach, and it will be given him." James 1:5

Your genius won't look like anyone else's. And sometimes you may feel doubtful that you have any—especially if you get stuck comparing your level of development to others. Be patient and kind with yourself, and enjoy the skills you have. Ask God to bring to your attention new ways you can grow your talents and wisdom. He will answer that request (John 14:13-13, John 15:16, James 1:5).

He loves you right where you are today, and He will use your talents to positively impact others all your life.

Spiritual Gifts

One of the joys of redemption is that God deposits special and supernatural areas of ability in us, such as teaching, giving, encouraging, and showing mercy. A list of these spiritual gifts is found in Romans 12:3-8 and 1 Corinthians 12:4-11. Spiritual gifts are different from natural talents or interests. Their specific purposes are to lead people to a saving knowledge of Jesus and to strengthen the church, such as encouraging or teaching believers, for the ultimate purpose of bringing attention and praise to God.

"As each has received a gift, use it to serve one another, as good stewards of God's varied grace: whoever speaks, as one who speaks oracles of God; whoever serves, as one who serves by the strength that God supplies—in order that in everything God may be glorified through Jesus Christ."
1 Peter 4:10-11

You may sometimes feel tempted to envy others' gifts. Remember that these gifts are given to believers *by* God, for *His* glory. The goal is using them to lift God's name up, not our own. Comparing spiritual gifts to see who is most important is a misuse of our effort and energy. We are all handcrafted by God and needed in His kingdom.

To This Moment in Time

It's okay that you're still figuring out your strengths. The key to confidence is not "owning" your own skills or having every day mapped out perfectly. Confidence comes simply from knowing you are loved and wanted by God.

Scripture says Jesus could wash the disciples' feet because He knew who He was. The assurance that He was God's Son gave Him the courage and humility to do whatever was needed to complete the Father's work. Jesus wasn't looking for the crowd's approval. He wasn't waiting for His disciples to worship His almighty position. He wasn't living for anyone to like Him. So He took off His outer coat and postured Himself as a servant.

Jesus set an example when He washed the disciples' dirty feet. In this act, He taught us that in leading people, you communicate the most when you make yourself the least. Shortly after getting their feet washed, some of the disciples argued about who would be the greatest and where they would sit in heaven. Jesus pointed them back to their clean feet. He wanted them to get that life wasn't about being the best. It wasn't about superiority or position; it was about valuing others enough to serve them with the gospel. But we won't do that if we don't understand how He has rescued us and who He says we are.

When we know how loved we are—how wanted as His friend and child—something heals inside us. That assurance releases us from our mental grip on comparison. We finally stop insisting, "Prove to me that I'm good enough to be loved." We relax—we stop fighting the battle in our mind of despising ourselves instead of enjoying and accepting the life we have.

Like Jesus when He washed the disciples' feet, having a relationship with the Father is the place to start your journey of growth and service. Ask yourself, "To this moment in time, what has God shown me about Himself and myself? What am

I good at? What am I interested in? What is my rhythm/pace? What might He want me to do in the future? What are the needs of my neighbors and church?"

If God has shown you something to do, do it—even if you feel nervous or unprepared. Be obedient to what you know to this moment in time, because fruitfulness has way more to do with following Him than personal perfection.

As long as we have another day, we have another opportunity to become all He created us to be. Your fabulous combination of personality, growing character, natural talents and interests, and spiritual gifts is beyond compare. You have a place in His heart and an irreplaceable role in building His kingdom. So get up and go in His name!

CHAPTER 26

Knowing Where to Be

Wherever you are, you are there to tell the
Good News of Jesus.

Now an angel of the Lord said to Philip, "Rise and go
toward the south to the road that goes down from
Jerusalem to Gaza." This is a desert place. And he rose
and went. And there was an Ethiopian, a eunuch, a court
official of Candace, queen of the Ethiopians, who was in
charge of all her treasure. He had come to Jerusalem to
worship and was returning, seated in his chariot, and he
was reading the prophet Isaiah. And the Spirit said to
Philip, "Go over and join this chariot." So Philip ran to
him and heard him reading Isaiah the prophet and
asked, "Do you understand what you are reading?" And
he said, "How can I, unless someone guides me?" And he
invited Philip to come up and sit with him. Now the
passage of the Scripture that he was reading was this:
"...Like a lamb before its shearer is silent, so he opens
not his mouth...."

And the eunuch said to Philip, "About whom...does
the prophet say this...?" Then Philip opened his mouth,
and beginning with this Scripture he told him the good
news about Jesus. And...they came to some water, and
the eunuch said, "See, here is water! What prevents me
from being baptized?" And he commanded the chariot
to stop, and they both went down into the water, Philip
and the eunuch, and he baptized him. And when they
came up out of the water, the Spirit of the Lord carried
Philip away, and the eunuch...went on his way rejoicing.
But Philip found himself at Azotus, and...he preached the
gospel to all the towns until he came to Caesarea.

Acts 8:26-40

One of my daughters runs a successful online market featuring hand-lettered inspirational tees, greeting cards, and stickers*. She can draw about anything, and I'm constantly suggesting she make cards with cartoon animals and corny puns. When I describe my newest idea, she says, "Thanks for the idea, Mom, but no." From time to time, others ask her to create a product. She listens to every idea, but she's not afraid to say no to people's requests—even if they're willing to pay. At first, I didn't get why she didn't draw for my entertainment. In time, I understood why *no* had to be her default answer. If she spends time and money making what everyone else wants, she wouldn't reach *her* goal, which is creating products that help young women draw closer to God. Her *no* to me is her *yes* to the vision God planted in her heart.

Before my experience with her business, I didn't really understand why a person should be uncompromising. I mean, I said that about my faith—that as a Christian, I wouldn't let people pressure me into denying what I believe. But I thought of it as a defensive thing—I'd push back if I'm asked to compromise. I hadn't thought of it as an offensive move: that I should be so convinced of a direction that I immediately say no if something isn't within the goals God has shown me. It's not rude—saying no is necessary to get where He wants us to go. Our vision to honor Him with our lives is like cutting a path through the thick tangle of distractions the world offers. We should aim for the end like a laser.

How do we know when to say no and when to say yes? When to get up and go and when to stop and serve where we are? Sometimes we don't have direction strong enough to cut a path. We don't have a well-formulated purpose. Our goal is to please people or be part of the crowd, which makes our

*www.anneliwhitedesigns.com

default answer, "Yes," instead of, "Thanks for the idea, but no." We need courage to set God-led limits and follow Him on the path He's shown us. We need wisdom to know what that path is.

In Acts 8, an angel told Philip the location of a person who was searching for God. I love how Scripture says after the angel drops the address: "This is a desert place." Philip could have argued, "Who would be out in the middle of nowhere looking for salvation?" We know how to stall like that. I have certainly tried to argue with God about my lack of ability and that what He's asking is impossible and inconvenient. But when Philip got the address, the Bible says, "He rose and went." His response was *obedient* and *immediate*. He didn't ask God why. He didn't ask God how. He got up and walked where he was supposed to go. When Philip saw the chariot in the desert, he started getting to know the man. When the man asked him a question about the Scriptures, Philip, "opened his mouth, and… told him the good news." His courage resulted in the explanation of the gospel. In case you're tempted to say, "Well, he was one of those special ones," Philip was not one of the original 12 disciples. He was a Christ-follower like you and me.

I'll admit, determining the specifics of where He wants us to be is confusing sometimes. I wish we could type "God's will" into a search engine and come up with a plan for every day. The Bible records very few people having the experience of Philip, where an angel tells them the address of where to go or God's Spirit whisks them away to the next place of ministry. But we can learn to live with the attitude Philip had. We can get up and go without questioning God's lead, and we can open our mouth to boldly tell people about Jesus.

I think Philip could respond this resolutely because he had done the work of defining his purpose and choosing God to be the authority in His life. We spin our wheels because we haven't settled those things. We pray to be safe and provided for, but we fail to ask God, "Why did You put me on the earth?" Start asking Him that question. Write down specific goals He brings to mind, whether they center on character issues, sin struggles, ministry or service ideas, or people groups that need to hear about Him. Don't worry that you don't know every detail of your future; write what you do know. And don't worry if what you write looks like it won't lead to security and prosperity. It's time to trust Him.

Three things that help you discern God's direction happen to spell out ***map: m***ore time in His Word, ***a***ffirmation of circumstances and others, and ***p***rayer. Following these principles is a great way to map out your life.

More Time in His Word

We have been given God's Word, and that is the place to start when you're looking for specifics of what God wants you to do. What does He want you to study? Where does He want you to live? Whom does He want you to date? How does He want you to spend your money and time? Although God doesn't list your spouse's name in the Bible, He definitely gives clear guidance about every area of life. Through stories, direct instruction, and foundational principles, God reveals what's important to Him in Scripture: the nations hearing the Good News of Jesus, discipleship, speaking up for injustice, caring for poor people, the value of children, personal holiness, treasuring His Word, and so much more show up as His priorities.

God would never ask us to go against His commands or act opposite His heart toward others. If we haven't spent any time at all reading and considering His Word, or if we haven't listened to what He's already revealed to us, is it any wonder we are confused about our next steps? Our lives can't make an impact for Jesus Christ if we don't do anything He says, and we won't do what He says if we don't know what He says.

Often, we approach God's Word kind of daring it to speak to us. We think, "*If* it speaks to me today, I'll do something about it," and we rush through reading a verse or two. But Hebrews 4:12-13 explain that the Bible is alive and constantly speaking, drawing us close to God and teaching us to live for His glory. So before we start each day's activities, we should renew our commitment and enjoy fellowship with Him in His Word. We can assume He will speak to us every time we make time for it—what a privilege to be loved and shown attention in this way by the King of Kings.

"But if you look carefully into the perfect law that sets you free, and if you do what it says and don't forget what you heard, then God will bless you for doing it."
James 1:25, NLT

Sometimes we want to make a dramatic declaration that we will go wherever God leads—even to prison or death. Peter pledged that to Jesus in Luke 22:33, but before the end of the chapter, he denied knowing Him. We say, "Lord, I'll live for you," but we can't get to the end of the day without comparing, complaining, getting angry, being lazy, or giving in to our cravings. God isn't looking for a one-time proclamation. Love means everyday faithfulness, a lifelong series of yeses to His Lordship in big and little areas of life, including making an effort to know Him. Even if we don't know all the specifics of where life will take us, ultimately, our purpose is to know and glorify Him. We do that through studying His Words.

Affirmation of Circumstances and Others

Another indicator of direction might be what circumstances we are in or what others seem to be saying. God does naturally limit our choices through circumstances. This causes us to consider steps we may not have otherwise considered, and those turn out to be incredibly fruitful.

Another source of direction is the advice of Christian friends. God gives us wisdom and encouragement from fellow believers. He uses people to point out things we didn't know we were good at or to reassure us when we're feeling insecure. If you are actively asking God, He may answer your request for what next steps to consider through the affirmation of others or circumstances—but use caution in leaning on this as your only determining factor in making decisions.

Circumstances and people's input are placed between the bookends of God's Word and prayer because we take our direction from **God**, not human opinion or coincidence. Sometimes we use these to justify what we want instead of waiting to hear from God—like if a job or relationship we know deep down we're not supposed to take is offered with lots of sign-on bonuses, we say the open door must mean it is God's will.

When circumstances line up, this does not necessarily mean we should walk through that "open" door. Sometimes God actually wants us to choose to walk away. The first open door may not be the one He has for us. And a closed door may not mean "no." It may mean *keep knocking*, instead of *walk away.* God can use trials and delays to help us grow in grit and to learn more about Him, so don't be afraid of imperfect circumstances. Sometimes God wants us to tackle the hard or risky thing.

Prayer

Sometimes we credit God for a direction or possession He's never been consulted about—we made the decision based only on circumstances then say it must be God's will. Before making any move in life, we need to learn what it means to pray. Prayer is talking to God about everything, even questioning Him, and taking the time to listen. We can ask Him for clear direction, and we can ask Him to move mountains that are in the way of the path He has shown us.

The more we pray, the more we learn to recognize what people sometimes call His still, small voice. That's a human way of trying to describe the gentle tug or corrective nudge of the Holy Spirit. If you haven't practiced talking with Him about your decisions, now is the time to start.

> "And this is the confidence that we have toward him, that if we ask anything according to his will he hears us."
> 1 John 5:14

Living to make God's love and grace known to others will require great courage. In a day where young women rarely look past present popularity, material gain, and how much they can compromise and still be "safe" spiritually, you can bravely ask, "Lord, teach me what do You want me to do. Help me define my purpose. Let my life bring You glory." And you can bravely go where He leads in His name.

DECISION-MAKING QUESTIONS

Use these questions as you consider priorities and goals.

- Are you willing to follow God's lead and serious about hearing what He wants you to do?
- What does the Bible say about this pursuit?
- What kind of person would you like to be?
- What would you like to be remembered for?
- Is this the right timing?
- What does this decision communicate about my belief in God's authority?
- What does this communicate about who/what is at the center of my life (what drives me)?
- What natural consequences might result from this decision?
- How will I handle the criticism of others related to this decision?
- Am I making this decision to please others, to please myself, or to please God?
- Does this decision align with my long-term goals?
- Which will you regret more—doing it or not doing it?
- What are you saying *yes* to that should be eliminated?
- What is the first thing you would do for others if you had a million dollars? Can you do a version of that— the core of it—with the resources you currently have?
- Are you solving a problem (for yourself or others) if you move forward with the pursuit—or will it create more problems?

CHAPTER 27
Oaks Who Build

Building up another person's esteem doesn't tear down your own.

Now a Jew named Apollos, a native of Alexandria, came to Ephesus. He was an eloquent man, competent in the Scriptures. He had been instructed in the way of the Lord. And being fervent in spirit, he spoke and taught accurately the things concerning Jesus, though he knew only the baptism of John. He began to speak boldly in the synagogue, but when Priscilla and Aquila heard him, they took him aside and explained to him the way of God more accurately. And when he wished to cross to Achaia, the brothers encouraged him and wrote to the disciples to welcome him. When he arrived, he greatly helped those who through grace had believed, for he powerfully refuted the Jews in public, showing by the Scriptures that the Christ was Jesus.

Acts 18:24-28

I still remember trying to memorize my first Bible verses, John 14:2-3. The long passage seemed daunting to me as a second grader. I would say a word or two without looking at my Sunday School take-home paper, then peek to make sure I had it right. Again and again I wrestled to get the phrases right in my head. I wouldn't have tried so much, but I *loved* my Sunday School teacher, Mrs. Barbara Whitehouse. I had just moved from Michigan to Kentucky. I didn't want to leave my friends and the little farm where I grew up in a snowy wonderland, but this one lady made all the difference—I wanted to grow up and be like her. So when she asked me in her gentle way if I could try to say the verses in class the next week, I *tried*. Mrs. Whitehouse, also known as "The Praying Lady," has been an oak in my life ever since. She celebrated my high school graduation with my family and attended my wedding. She prayed with me when I was looking for my first job, and, many years later, still encourages me to do what God has prepared me for—what *she* helped prepare me for. She would never take any credit, though. In her life, conversations, and relationships, she gives the praise to God.

What are oaks? As you can imagine, their character and motivations are the opposite of ivy. Their desire is to give life, not snatch it. They live to advance others and God's kingdom, not to promote or keep things for themselves. They nurture faith and provide shelter for healing souls. They point people to Jesus. An oak isn't always someone with a huge platform. God certainly uses people with a large reach to speak for Him. But oaks are also people who serve faithfully in local communities all over the world—they are making a direct investment into people. They may lead churches, classes, or organizations in visible ways, or, unseen, they pray at home. No one ever knows the battle some Christians fight for fellow believers on their knees. Oaks may be family and friends, and sometimes people you've met only once. They live near and far away. They can be those who visit prisons, or the incarcerated in prisons. Those who have walked blamelessly, or those who have made huge mistakes. God uses all kinds of people to encourage the next generation of His people to see His glory. We all need oaks in our lives, and we can become oaks to others.

"Blessed is the man who walks not in the counsel of the wicked, nor stands in the way of sinners, nor sits in the seat of scoffers; but his delight is in the law of the Lord, and on his law he meditates day and night. He is like a tree planted by streams of water that yields its fruit in its season, and its leaf does not wither. In all that he does, he prospers. The wicked are not so, but are like chaff that the wind drives away."
Psalm 1:1-4

"I don't know anyone like that, someone who wants to help my progress and isn't absorbed with his or her own," you may say. It's true that oaks are a rare treasure, but God has raised up many people to help His children grow. Maybe you haven't met one because you haven't looked for one yet. Be careful with whom you spend your time. Psalm 1 explains that we have a choice whose counsel we listen to. We can hang around with people who value God's Word or laugh at it. Since it's pretty common that we become like those we spend time with, choose well whom you admire. Ask God to help you find the right mentors and friends. Look for people with proven character and deep faith that you would like to have.

In Acts 18, we meet a couple you may have heard of before, Aquila and Priscilla. (Isn't it cute that their names rhyme? Don't confuse them with Ananias and Sapphira!) They worked together making tents and making disciples. They met a young preacher named Apollos. He was a Jew and had a special gift of explaining the Scriptures. Aquila and Priscilla noticed he had distinctive skills but needed to learn more about Jesus so that he could explain God more clearly. Instead of criticizing Apollos behind his back and complaining that he was trying to do something he wasn't fully equipped for, they came alongside him, told him they saw his talents, and gave their time to prepare him for the ministry they knew he would have. Oaks are like that—they often see what you can do before you do.

After Priscilla and Aquila discipled Apollos, he was ready to travel and preach to others. The Bible says that the leaders of the church wrote a letter to endorse him. Even in church, people are tempted to whittle a sharp spear of competition, poking at one another. But when even a couple of people set a tone of supportive mentorship, it can help an entire church, protecting them from internal jealousy that can crumble a strong foundation.

Oaks teach us to affirm others' gifts. They help us remember that *more* people—not an exceptional few—need to be involved in sharing the gospel. When believers treat one another right, it greatly helps unbelievers—mentorship serves as an example of God's love, as well as teaching more people practical skills to reach others with the gospel.

You may not have realized it, but *you* are also part of God's plan for encouraging His body of believers. You may feel young and uninfluential, but your courage to choose holiness and be kind in Jesus' name makes a huge imprint on others' lives. First Timothy 4:12 says you can set an example in speech, behavior, life, love, and purity. You can live like an oak right now. God created you for this.

> "For we are his workmanship, created in Christ Jesus for good works... that we should walk in them."
> Ephesians 2:10

So often, we ignore the opportunity we have each day to affirm others. Our insecurity about our impact doesn't negate the reality that our words can change lives. We all know that rancid words of bitter people wound deeply. The words linger in others' minds and bring about lasting pain. Even though the source of the words is thoroughly untrustworthy, we can't un-hear and ignore their opinions. Likewise, a simple, sincere word of encouragement, even from someone younger or with less experience, can change the course of another person's day. Like Aquila and Priscilla, we change people's lives when we change their attitude toward themselves and remind them of the forgiveness of Jesus.

While we don't live for the approval of others, giving and receiving affirmation is part of being a trusted friend. Affirmation is more than saying compliments. It includes describing the value and gifts you see in another person and helping a person understand the Bible more clearly.

Most of the world is afraid to say the good they see in others—they fear it takes something away from their personhood. But building up another person's esteem doesn't tear down your own. In many ways, it strengthens it. Here are some practical ways to be an oak—a wise friend and encourager. These don't have to be done all at once—they are ideas to practice over a lifetime!

- Notice what people are good at, and tell them.

- After interacting with someone, make notes about their worries and interests in your journal. Pray specifically and regularly for their needs.

- Write notes expressing what people mean to you. One technique is to title the note, "Without You," and write ways that person makes a positive difference in the world.

- Make a friend record book. Use an address book that has several lines for each entry—record the name of each friend, gifts you have given or would like to give the person; favorite interests and Bible verses; and things you'd like to do with or for the person. Look at the book when it's time to write a note or celebrate a special occasion.

- Dedicate a mini-notebook to support one person. As God leads, write prayers for that person. Clearly mark the date of your prayers. When you fill it, give it to the person as a way to let them know that someone has been praying for them over time.

- Support your friends in practical ways—go to their games and events, remember their concerns and interests, give a card on their birthdays, and comment positive words on their posts (not every post—but sometimes do more than tap the heart).

- Watch your expectations of others and yourself—don't feel unworthy because you can't do more. Be who you are, do what you can, and don't expect more than you should from friends.

- Point them to Christ. In addition to encouragement, one of the greatest purposes of human friendship is for us to remind each other of God's love.

- Laugh, play, and eat together. Learn a new skill together, like cooking or barre. Reach a goal together, like running a mini-marathon.

- Work together for causes greater than yourselves. Friendship feeds our need for comfort and acceptance, but we can also use it to benefit those outside our circle. Things like going to Bible study, working at a volunteer agency, and serving on mission teams strengthen ties and build memories.

- Include new people. It's easy to stick primarily with old friends, even at places like church. Consider how others might feel if you interact only with favorite friends. Widen your circle—include new friends for a walk, makeover night, or movie outing. You never know how your invitation might change someone's outlook.

- Ask an older woman for input. Someone in a different age category might seem intimidating, but don't be afraid to occasionally ask women you admire to host a cooking or craft night, to lead a study on a topic your friends have questions about, or to share advice on areas they have more experience with. You might find a forever friend by doing this!

- Be serious about praying for your friends, believers and unbelievers. God hears our cries, and *no one other than you may be praying for some people in your circle*.

CHAPTER 28

Get Up! Let's Go!

Be brave enough to go where God leads—without comparison.

The people of Israel cried out to the Lord for help, for he had 900 chariots of iron and he oppressed the people of Israel cruelly for twenty years.

Now Deborah, a prophetess, the wife of Lappidoth, was judging Israel at that time. She used to sit under the palm of Deborah between Ramah and Bethel in the hill country of Ephraim, and the people of Israel came up to her for judgment. She sent and summoned Barak ... and said to him, "Has not the Lord, the God of Israel, commanded you, 'Go, gather your men at Mount Tabor, taking 10,000 from the people of Naphtali and the people of Zebulun. And I will draw out Sisera, the general of Jabin's army, to meet you by the river Kishon with his chariots and his troops, and I will give him into your hand'?" Barak said to her, "If you will go with me, I will go, but if you will not go with me, I will not go." And she said, "I will surely go with you...."

Deborah said to Barak, "Up! For this is the day in which the Lord has given Sisera into your hand. Does not the Lord go out before you?" So Barak went down from Mount Tabor with 10,000 men following him. And the Lord routed Sisera and all his chariots and all his army before Barak by the edge of the sword.

Judges 4:3-9, 14-15

I worked on this book for 10 years. I could say it shouldn't have taken so long, but the time it took was purposeful. The Lord formulated the ideas, and I taught the Bible passages to several groups of women and loved gaining their insights. I made notes while I raised my four kids and served in my jobs. At times, I made excuses to mask my fear that I couldn't communicate what His Word teaches. But when I felt like God was saying, "Now," I resigned my job and sat at my writing desk, my cat beside me, and prayed and wrestled hard with words and insecurities until I could share His love in this printed way.

The timing and work of God is fascinating. Sometimes He acts immediately. Sometimes He delays on purpose. Sometimes He acts outside the bounds of natural and possible happenings. Sometimes He works through ordinary people. God asks us to do things in areas where we are naturally competent. He also asks us to do things in areas where we feel inexperienced and incompetent. He has a reason for all He does. He doesn't want anything—sin, expectations, fear, insecurity, or even ability—to steal His glory. So when He says, "Go," it's time to get up and get going.

In Judges 4, Deborah urges Barak to lead troops of Israelites against an oppressive dictator. She tells Barak this is what God wants him to do. It is unclear whether she was explaining his job for the first time or reminding him of something he already knew and was stalling about. He said he would do the work if she went with him. (Having a collaborator in ministry often gives us the encouragement we need to start and finish something.) The morning of the battle, Deborah told Barak, "It's time to go." Again, it's unclear if he was stalling, but it seems like she had to do a lot of prodding to get him to move. Maybe I recognize it because

I have also delayed. What convinces him to *go* is these words: "Does not the Lord go out before you?"

The assurance that God is with us shrinks our fears and moves us forward. Let's look at a couple heroes of the faith to whom God promised His presence and see how they reacted.

Joshua

"'Just as I was with Moses, so I will be with you. I will not leave you or forsake you. Be strong and courageous, for you shall cause this people to inherit the land that I swore to their fathers to give them....This Book of the Law shall not depart from your mouth, but you shall meditate on it day and night, so that you may be careful to do according to all that is written in it. For then you will make your way prosperous, and then you will have good success. Have I not commanded you? Be strong and courageous. Do not be frightened, and do not be dismayed, for the Lord your God is with you wherever you go.'

"And Joshua commanded the officers of the people, 'Pass through the midst of the camp and command the people, "Prepare your provisions, for within three days you are to pass over this Jordan to go in to take possession of the land that the Lord your God is giving you to possess."'"
Joshua 1:5-11

Daniel

"Again one having the appearance of a man touched me and strengthened me. And he said, 'O man greatly loved, fear not, peace be with you; be strong and of good courage.' And as he spoke to me, I was strengthened."
Daniel 10:18-19

Don't miss what God is doing here. Joshua and Daniel ended up doing the work God had for them, but they didn't start out feeling very confident. Remember, Moses didn't either (see Chapter 6). In each of these scenes, they were wrestling with fear: of people's opinions and of the obstacles they were up against. In these real-life scenarios, God's people were being hurt by cruel enemies. His people cried for deliverance, and He heard. Sometimes God supernaturally intervenes to stop human pain, but, more often, He raises up a human to move a group to action, and their leadership results in rescue and relief. The human is never qualified or deserving to do God's work. *Never, no matter who it is.* Naturally, when God asks us to do something, we feel insecure. Without His help, it is true that we are not capable of success that impacts people for an eternity. It feels frightening to walk into enemy territory, uncertain of victory and inexperienced in battle tactics. Even Joshua and Daniel were scared, but God didn't shame them. He also did not pump them up with a fluff reply. His answer was not, "Aw, you can do it! Find your power within. You've got what it takes.'" God's answer every time was a promise and a revelation: "I will be with you. You are weak, but I am able."

God provided this reassurance through coworkers, angels, and a direct message from Himself. He speaks the same message today to fill us with the peace and courage we need to move forward in spite of fear: "I will be with you."

So many times when someone is good at something we aren't good at, we say, "I can't do that," and shut down. When we are challenged to start something new, we assume, "I can't learn that," and don't even try. When we see oppressors hurting others, we shiver, "I can't overcome them," and we let the bullying continue. The problem with these answers is that they start with "I." If we haven't learned anything else in our time together, maybe we've learned this: *God can*. Our lives are about what God has done and will do. We find our confidence and courage in experiencing His presence and enjoying His love. We find our abilities when we know Him.

> "And when the sixth hour had come, there was darkness over the whole land until the ninth hour. And at the ninth hour Jesus cried with a loud voice, "...My God, my God, why have you forsaken me?"... And Jesus uttered a loud cry and breathed his last.... And the curtain of the temple was torn in two, from top to bottom."
> Mark 15:33-34, 38

For one moment in time, Jesus experienced the opposite of the presence God has promised us. It was the moment when the sin of all of humanity was heaped on Him and He paid for it with the greatest punishment anyone can ever experience—separation from God. In that moment, He bought us the opportunity to fellowship with God.

It is no small thing that the curtain of the temple tore from top to bottom when Jesus died. In Exodus 26, in His instructions for construction of the temple, God gave the design for this virtually indestructible panel to separate sinful people from His divine presence. Only the high priest could pass through it into the Holy of Holies. When God turned His face from our sin—and His Son who carried it—the most sacred place of connection became open to us. We no longer have to remain separated from our Creator. Because of Jesus, we have assurance that we can enter His presence (Ephesians 3:12; Hebrews 4:16).

It is a privilege to be loved so deeply. Knowing we are loved eases our fear that we will fail and be rejected. We can get up and go without the weight of insecurity dragging us down. God loves and uses people who are unimportant, weak, and insignificant in the world's eyes. So now that we know He meets us where we are, the question remains: do we believe His promises that we are beyond compare?

You are competent, not compared.
You are significant, not stunted.
You are accepted, not the object of anger.
You are wanted, not less-than.
You are gifted, not incapable.
You are irreplaceable, not uninteresting.
You are precious and treasured by the King of Kings.

Let us then with confidence
draw near to the throne of grace,
that we may receive mercy and find grace
to help in time of need.
Hebrews 4:16

ACKNOWLEDGEMENTS

Thanks to long-time friends Terri, Rachel, Melissa S., Vanessa, Devin, the Shannons, Shephards, Yanceys, Barretts, Doyles, Heddens, Ballards, and Hobsons, George, Eduardo, Cindy, Ashley, Carmon, Mary, Kathie, and a host of others who have given me encouragement and opportunities. My precious husband Jwain and loving children Marina (and Mason), Samuel, Ruthie (and Grant), and Anneli are great editors and even better friends. I also treasure the thoughts of my extended family. Thank you for supporting me. Special thanks to Jeremy and Sharon White; Jenaye White, publicist; and Myriah Snyder, editor, for their investment of time and resources in this project.